CONFLICT : VIOLENCE
AND NONVIOLENCE

The Editor

J O A N V. B O N D U R A N T is Professor of
Politics at Callison College of the University of
the Pacific and a Fellow of the Institute of International Studies at the University of California,
Berkeley. She was awarded her bachelor's degree
by the University of Michigan and her doctorate
by the University of California, Berkeley. After
having spent many years in India, her professional career reflects a dual line of interest in
conflict and conflict resolution, on the one hand,
and, on the other, South Asia studies with
emphasis on the government and politics of India. Dr. Bondurant is the author of *Conquest of
Violence: The Gandhian Philosophy of Conflict*
and has contributed numerous articles to scholarly
publications on the subjects of political and
social change in South Asia, Indian political
thought, and problems of conflict and conflict
resolution. She has served as Chairman of the
Center for South Asia Studies for the Institute
of International Studies on the Berkeley campus
and as Associate Editor of the Indian Press
Digests.

CONFLICT:

EDITED BY

L

VIOLENCE AND NONVIOLENCE

Joan V. Bondurant

IN ASSOCIATION WITH
Margaret W. Fisher

LIEBER-ATHERTON

New York 1973

CONFLICT: VIOLENCE AND NONVIOLENCE
edited by Joan V. Bondurant

Copyright © 1971 by Aldine • Atherton, Inc.

Address all inquiries to:
Lieber-Atherton, Incorporated
1841 Broadway
New York, New York 10023

Library of Congress Catalog Card Number 71-116543
ISBN 0-88311-011-3 (cloth); 0-88311-012-1 (paper)

Second Printing 1973

Printed in the United States of America

Preface

The political scientist may well begin his inquiry into conflict by questioning whether there is anything in politics that is *not* conflict-centered. Yet that question soon gives way to an even more fundamental consideration, for, in some sense, all of man's efforts may be said to arise from conflict. The need for continuing resolution of conflict within the self, the search for avenues through which human animosities can be controlled as individual interacts with individual, the design of devices with which competing interests are contained in society—all these aspects of conflict are reflected in a vast and substantial body of literature that extends well beyond the social sciences.

But what of violence and nonviolence, the two contrasting modes for conducting conflict? What do man's reflections have to tell us about these? And how do they relate to contemporary problems? If one begins his inquiry at this point in the formula and if he seeks to go behind polemics to more serious concern with systematic efforts put forward to resolve the persistent and unyielding problems of conflict, he comes up against a poverty of relevant material. Theories of conflict are few, as are theoretical formulations relating to violence. And if one presses the search forward to include analyses of nonviolence, he comes upon a field that, for the most part, still lies fallow.

An attempt has been made here to bring together essays written by scholars in this field who are concerned with contemporary problems. None of these essays (including three written specifically for this volume) purports to be definitive. They are presented here in the hope that they will provide some base for further inquiry into conflict and alternative methods for its conduct. Especially because of the unevenness of extant literature, it is not only to be expected but also to be desired that such a compilation will raise more questions than it answers.

In an effort to present as much relevant material as possible, passages from many of the original essays have been omitted. In each such case the opening page carries the foot notation "abridged." I am grateful to copyright holders for granting permission to make necessary cuts. (In only one of the essays have elision marks been shown, by explicit request.) An earnest effort has been made to keep to the argument. Omitted material is usually illustrative or in the nature of elaboration.

Acknowledgment should be made, first of all, to the University of California, Berkeley, with which both editors have long been affiliated. The University's Institute of International Studies supported the research and writing of this book; the Department of Political Science provided valuable research assistance.

An extensive debt of gratitude is owed to many colleagues and friends who contributed to the fashioning of this book. Professor David Spitz, the general editor of this series, not only made significant suggestions but also extended warm and constant encouragement. Dr. Portia Bell Hume authenticated the material borrowed from the field of psychiatry and stimulated insights that led to several lines of argument appearing in my own essays.

My thanks are due all the authors whose work is represented here. I am especially grateful to Professors Gene Sharp and E. V. Walter, whose enthusiasm refreshed and sustained me at critical phases in the work. During the early selective processing of extensive literature, Mr. James T. Burnett served as an excellent and resourceful research assistant.

I wish to make special acknowledgment of the many contributions by my colleague, Dr. Margaret W. Fisher. She encouraged the undertaking of this work, collaborated in every phase of the editing, and contributed the concluding essay.

Contents

Preface   ix

The Search for a Theory of Conflict   1
JOAN V. BONDURANT

I   Familiar Modes of Nonviolence

1 : *The New Peace Movement*   29
ROY FINCH

2 : *The New Pacifism*   45
STEPHAN THERNSTROM

3 : *Limits to the Moral Claim in Civil Disobedience*   50
HARRY PROSCH

4 : *The Moral Ground of Civil Disobedience*   62
DARNELL RUCKER

II   Forms and Uses of Violence

5 : *The Threat of Violence and Social Change*   73
H. L. NIEBURG

6 : *Violence and the Process of Terror*   89
EUGENE V. WALTER

III   Symbolic Violence or Creative Conflict?

7 : *Evolution and Revolution*   111
ERNEST JONES

8 : *Creative Conflict and the Limits of Symbolic
      Violence*   120
JOAN V. BONDURANT

IV   Is There an Alternative to Violence?

9 : *Fractionating Conflict*   135
ROGER FISHER

10 : *Comments on "Fractionating Conflict"*   146
LAWRENCE S. FINKELSTEIN

11 : *The Technique of Nonviolent Action*   151
GENE SHARP

12 : *Some Questions on Civilian Defense*   172
THOMAS C. SCHELLING

V   Epilogue

13 : *Contrasting Approaches to Conflict*   183
MARGARET W. FISHER

Index   203

CONFLICT : VIOLENCE
AND NONVIOLENCE

The Search for a Theory of Conflict

JOAN V. BONDURANT

From futile day through uncreative night
to futile day we carry as a load
the powers that could be used, the thoughts that might
transcend the cycle, the means to free the node.
It is for us to look, and looking see,
and seeing think, and do, and doing be.[1]

The idea of conflict has dominated intellectual history throughout the centuries. Whatever the immediate focus of man's reflections, the entire fabric of political thought has been woven around problems of human conflict, conflict between individuals and groups as they relate to one another in society. What is the cause of conflict and how is it to be expressed? These are central considerations. But perhaps the most serious consideration of all is the problem of how conflict can be controlled.

Because violence has been the primary mode of conducting conflict, the literature of political theory is replete with argu-

1

ments justifying, explaining, analyzing, and defining force. Usually, but not always, force is taken to be essentially violent. Indeed, the study of politics might well begin with an exploration of the concept of conflict and of its primary manifestation in violence. It cannot end there, for in more recent times those strands of thought that seek to deal with conflict in ways that would minimize or eliminate violence have taken a new turning. Still overshadowed by other compelling arguments, the case for nonviolence, and especially for nonviolent action, has come to highlight the over-arching problem, conflict itself.

Consider the following constellation of questions:

Is conflict inevitable? This is a question about human nature and the point at which so much classical political thought begins.

How are men to be governed? Once the human-nature position is established, a solution to this question is sought through the fashioning of devices by which conflict of interest can be resolved (or, at times, denied).

Is society to be distinguished from the state, and, if so, what is the role of the state? From these interrelated questions issue conflict theories that seek to explain the state's origin as well as the many approaches to revolution and to political obligation.

How is conflict to be contained? Law, it is often argued, is the means through which society gives to the state a monopoly of violent means, and its purpose is to delimit destructive force.

How is conflict to be conducted? The highly developed concept of power as well as the several notions about influence center here.[2]

These are key questions for the political philosopher. That there is no single answer to any of them, if not self-evident, is demonstrated by the posing of the problems from age to age. In selecting the articles that make up the body of this book, an attempt has been made to serve the needs of the reader who asks his questions of contemporary trends and who seeks for what might be new in the posing of age-old questions in the current context, especially as they have aroused continued recourse to violence and have inspired new experiments with nonviolence for conducting conflict over current issues.

The well-informed student of political theory will note many omissions in this book, for the works of distinguished and classical philosophers on questions of war, peace, and conflict—from the early Greeks to Hobbes, Rousseau, Machiavelli, Kant, Bagehot, Sorel, Clausewitz, and on to the more recent studies of such scholars as Quincy Wright and Hannah Arendt or the contributions of popular leaders of whom the late Martin Luther King, Jr., is the most distinguished—are noted only fleetingly in references made to them by the contemporary scholars included here.[3] The eminent and classic works are omitted not because they have no relevance today but because there is much that is compelling in the proposition that all that has gone before— whether viewed in terms of competing ideas or of varying explications of the same problem, whether taken altogether or factored out in an effort to demonstrate the relevance of respective concepts or constructs—has failed to change man's intensive involvement with destruction.

The reader is invited to question this statement, just as he must probe and question the propositions that emerge from the contrasting essays in the body of this book. He would do well to carry a few constant questions to the reading of each part: What are the normative considerations of each author, that is, to what value system is each author's argument related? If nonviolence is to be preferred to violence, what, if anything, would be lost in the application of proposals presented here? Is the author predisposed *against* violence because it is destructive or because he fears conflict itself? Is there an attraction *to* violence because significant aspects of conflict have not been recognized?

My own preferences (or biases) become clear not only because I argue that it is imperative for mankind to develop a new conceptual framework within which new techniques can be fashioned for the active conduct of conflict but also through the selection and arrangement of the essays presented. I hold that the most neglected area in the study of social conflict is one that I have discussed in chapter 8, "Creative Conflict and the Limits of Symbolic Violence" (pp. 120–132). Much that passes for nonviolence is, I submit, symbolic violence. And if we are to advance beyond the classical theorists, we must also press beyond positions, concepts, strategies, and tactics that attract wide attention on the contemporary scene. We must start with man as he is, but we must go forward to devise means to deal constructively with what is surely inevitable conflict. To break new ground is imperative.

What, then, are the prominent threads in the fabric of contemporary approaches to conflict in its several forms? We begin in Part I with pacifism and civil disobedience, the most familiar modes of nonviolence.

PACIFISM AND CIVIL DISOBEDIENCE

The authors of the first two essays raise seminal questions about pacifism and point to new developments in the peace movements of our times. "Was not nonviolence just as potentially coercive as violence?" asks Roy Finch. In discussing the manner in which pacifists attempt to grapple with this and other questions, he touches upon the Gandhian position that nonviolence should be a matter of principle (and not merely one of technique), a principle to which at least the leadership must be committed.[4] This requires a degree of self-control that could be expected from only a select few. In following the pacifist consideration of Gandhian methods, Finch quickly comes to the problem of how means and ends are to be related.

The ends–means nexus is of such great significance that any commentary on conflict must be approached with questions about this central relationship. Does the end justify the means? Do the means determine or only condition the ends? Is it essential to proceed with an end objective in mind—or is process alone sufficient? Hannah Arendt (in a recent article not included here[5]) is no doubt correct when she states that violence is "instrumental by nature" and an actor never knows just what consequences his act will have. But what of her further argument that "violence can remain rational only if it pursues short-term goals"? Perhaps she answers that question when she concludes that "action is irreversible" and "a return to the status quo in case of defeat is always unlikely."

Both Finch and Thernstrom address themselves to the problem of the ends–means relationship—a problem of concern not only for those who hold pacifist positions but also for those who defend violence as a necessary means. The first essay grapples with the significant relationship of means to policy and raises hard questions about the political implications of the pacifist position.[6] Finch's theme that "automatic action and emotion" are substituted for thought and communication is elaborated upon in Part III by the late distinguished psychoanalyst Ernest Jones. One pauses to consider how much of the action in protest movements of our times arises out of sheer feeling, untempered by reflective thought and ill-prepared with knowledge.

Throughout the Finch essay, revolution—as political change —provides a focal point. Neither peace nor revolution makes a program, the argument runs, as it points up anomalies in some of the political positions taken by those who support "peace" candidates for political office.

The central theme in Finch's essay is that peace itself is the most urgent need. But can peace successfully be pursued merely by efforts to reverse the trend toward war, as is argued? Or does it rather require the fashioning of positive alternatives for the actual conduct of conflict? These questions are only occasionally raised in conflict studies, and they define the limited scope of the study of conflict in its status as a field of inquiry. Later in this introductory essay I shall press for the extension of inquiry into conflict to encompass and even to focus upon alternatives to violence.

In Chapter 2, "The New Pacifism," Thernstrom tends to agree with Finch's argument that too much emphasis is placed upon means by pacifists who hold that "bad" means cannot be used successfully for "good" ends. He goes on to reason that "it is false to insist that lesser-evil calculations must never be made in politics" and points out the undeniable fact that we cannot rid ourselves of painful choices for the important reason that there will always be basic competing values. He concludes that there will be times when one must choose "not peace but freedom and equality."

How, then, are freedom and equality to be secured when policies appear to infringe upon individual or civil rights? Until the more recent proliferation of modes of demonstration, many of which are violent, if only symbolically so, the most popular method short of violence has been civil disobedience. Any consideration of civil disobedience brings one directly to the many interlocking themes that cluster around the meaning and import of the law. Is there a law "higher" than the positive law constructed by man? This question brings us to yet another question in moral philosophy, and it is this key question that Harry Prosch explores lucidly in Chapter 3. He points out that in civil disobedience the moral claim is made through action, not merely in words. Because it is made through action, civil disobedience is often perceived as a power move forcing involvement upon those who would prefer not to take a stand. Such persons are cast in the role of supporting the laws being disobeyed whether or not they really believe in them. In this way conflict is joined not only by the avowed defenders of the law but also by those who have thought of themselves as innocent bystanders. This is so because they are forced to make a choice in a contest of force, a contest in which they would prefer not to be involved. Prosch points to the risk of engaging in civil disobedience and to the difficulties of bringing such disobedience to fruition as well as to the penalties for failure. He speaks to the question of justice and asks how one is to determine what is "right," giving attention to the ethical consequences of deciding what is "right" when one acts upon that decision.

In Chapter 4 Darnell Rucker joins the argument on civil disobedience and takes issue with Prosch, who, he tells us, confuses *civil* disobedience with defiance of the law. Rucker makes the cogent point that civil disobedience recognizes two essential demands of man's nature in social relationships: the right of the individual to choose what he wishes to do and his obligation to abide by whatever legal consequence may be imposed upon him as a result of his choice. But is civil disobedience necessarily nonviolent for the reason Rucker gives: that violence against the law and its officers of enforcement is rebellion or crime and is it not the purpose of civil disobedience to challenge the legality of a law or to ascertain the meaning of a law? He states the compelling considerations that one never knows how effective his action is going to be before he acts and that no man ever truly knows that any moral judgment is right. Nevertheless, a man must act on the basis of his moral judgments, using his own experience and evaluation of that experience which, in a free and well-ordered society, will cause him to hesitate in asserting his judgment as over against that embodied in the laws.[7] The further point that the preponderance of power will always lie with the government and that a reasonable man will weigh the importance of the issues at stake against the probable consequence of his open disobedience brings us to similar considerations for those who would use violence.[8]

VIOLENCE AND SYMBOLIC VIOLENCE

Radical social change is often linked with violence, as though the end to be sought necessitates the specific means of violence. The questions to raise here are those of imperatives on the one hand and efficacy on the other. The revolutionary readily turns to destructive acts to achieve his ends; the radical may well argue that only through violence can change be brought about. It is the philosophical anarchist who gives us the best clarification of the inherent problem, for, as I have suggested in my essay in Part III (pp. 120–132), the anarchist is caught in the dilemma of having to resort to violence to overcome what he views to be the violent, coercive nature of the state. When he acts he is driven to use the very means that he professes to disdain and for which he seeks a solution.

The anarchist dilemma is one of classic proportions. Whenever anarchist thought has emerged into anarchical deed, violence has been its close companion, for the anarchist has not overcome his dilemma however much he may have wished his objective to prevail over violence. Only the nihilist engages in violence for an immediate destructive purpose with what amounts to little more than a hope of some better form of social organization arising at some unknown future time and with little concern for either ends or means.

There are, however, yet other approaches to the use of violence, subtler in form and compelling in argument, to which Nieburg and Walter address themselves in Chapters 5 and 6.

As has been observed elsewhere, it is untrue that violence settles nothing. Nieburg argues that the *threat* of violence performs the function of inducing flexibility and stability in democratic institutions. The *possibility* of a violent revolution against the state may well arise with every generation, and the recognition of this possibility serves as a solvent for political rigidity, thus making revolution unnecessary. For the threat of violence and the fear of the breakdown of law and order "cast their shadow ahead."[9] This argument is also used with respect to potential international conflict where the credible threat of violence has a deterrent effect tending toward stabilization and, therefore, toward the maintenance of peace.

It is essential to make the all-important distinctions between the uses of violence within a totalitarian state and a democratic state, for it is just such distinctions that so graphically set the two polities at an extreme distance from each other. As Nieburg points out, the totalitarian approach is to intervene at the earliest possible moment to deflect or crush potential violence from any source of opposition; for this reason the threat of violence cannot be socially effective. In democratic states violence is tolerated to a point where it can have a social effect; initial violence is allowed to emerge from the pluralistic base so characteristic of democratic polity.[10] Usually, Nieburg observes, only token demonstration is necessary to effect a desired change. He extends his argument for risking violence to include "uncontrolled" and "irrational" violence in all its forms. A critical view of the limits of irrational violence is put forward in the two essays appearing in Part III.

The problem of terror no doubt does raise "virtually every other major issue in political sociology and political theory." This is the view of E. V. Walter in his essay "Violence and the Process of Terror" (Chap. 6). He addresses himself to the problem of power and argues that political systems legitimize certain kinds of potential violence—but within controlled limits. And this, he holds, is the meaning of force. A careful reading of Walter will clarify some misconceptions and faulty usages of concepts of power, force, punishment, and coercion, as well as of terror.[11] The threat of violence and the process of terror are extended to include their social effects, especially the emotional reaction of fear, which carries its own dysfunctional consequences.

When he argues that the mere presence of violence is not as significant as the degree of that violence, Walter touches upon one of the most significant considerations in the study of conflict. The place of violence in the service of power, the occasion for its official use, and even the necessity of violence in organized society are all germane. Here again one must distinguish between those systems that (1) use violence as a last resort and those in which (2) violence so extreme and so all-encompassing as to constitute terror is used as a first measure against those who would disagree with the system or those who would challenge it. Walter suggests a typology of power systems based on the manner in which they use violence.

The capacity to deal with terror is related to and based upon the understanding of fear. In his development and advocacy of satyagraha, Gandhi placed a high priority upon the requisite of what he called fearlessness. "I do believe," he wrote, "that where there is only a choice between cowardice and violence, I would advise violence." Gandhi insisted that nonviolent conduct is never demoralizing whereas cowardice always is.

Walter touches upon the need to uncover the hidden mechanisms in the human mind that account for the effectiveness of terror. This subject lies directly in the field of competence of Ernest Jones, who, in his essay "Evolution and Revolution" (Chap. 7), relates to styles of revolutionaries and their respective degrees of destructiveness. He draws upon his profound knowledge of human nature and his broad experience with personal histories to point out that some individuals engage in social action to work out their inner conflicting impulses as they attempt to deal with intrapsychic conflict. He raises the seminal question of why some revolutionaries are content to seize power and change social or political conditions "while others are possessed with a fury of destructiveness that cannot contemplate any continued existence of the things displaced." Again, he asks, "whence this bitter hatred and intolerance, the effects of which are always regretted by later generations who realize what they have lost forever?" Jones presents a psychological answer to this question and goes on to inquire into the nature of the idealistic and creative forces of evolutionary change.

In my own essay (Chap. 8) I use the Gandhian technique of satyagraha as a point of departure in contrasting the limited uses of symbolic violence with what I call creative conflict in an attempt to show that Gandhi began, but did not complete, the development of a technique for conducting conflict with a minimum of violence.

ALTERNATIVES TO VIOLENCE

Perhaps the most significant questions of all are raised, if not adequately answered, in Part IV, where certain alternatives to violence are broached. Roger Fisher's essay on fractionating conflict takes a step in pointing a direction for reducing conflict to manageable proportions in the international field by constructing proposals that, he argues, would effect the resolution of conflict. Lawrence Finkelstein challenges the Fisher argument, stressing the difficulties of treating conflict as an abstract concept. He argues that conflicts between states are too complex to yield to Fisher's solution, for they "involve the interaction of values, the perceptions and understandings of the actors, the means by which the conflict is conducted, the international political environment in which they occur, and the political processes and human relationships which affect the decisions of governmental leaders."

Questions about nonviolent alternatives are dealt with directly by Gene Sharp and Thomas Schelling in Chapters 11 and 12. The argument for an alternative to violence through a nonconventional approach to the control of political power is here set forth, in short compass, by Sharp. He argues for a defense policy that would deny to any enemy the "human assistance and cooperation which are necessary" if an invader "is to exercise control over the population." His definitions and discussion of such terms as "nonviolent action," "technique," "nonviolent intervention," and "nonviolent coercion" help clarify the argument. The recognition that "strategy is just as important in nonviolent action as it is in military action" leads to a serious consideration of the nature of conflict. Sharp's position is that conflict may indeed be conducted by combatants who fight but who do so with weapons quite different from those used by traditional military forces. He is suggesting a substitute for war that involves the wielding of power and the engaging of an invader by waging effective combat in a nonviolent way.

It is to be noted that Sharp's argument begins with the premise that the power of a ruler is dependent upon support from the people he would rule. It is this premise that Thomas Schelling concedes as he goes on to raise questions about the prospects of civilian defense. Schelling points out that disciplined unwillingness to comply does have a "unique defensive quality," for if it is successfully communicated it makes one "totally immune to threats." He then outlines the difficulties involved in supplanting military defense by nonviolent methods. His argument becomes intriguing indeed when he goes beyond "civilian defense" to explore its application to "civilian *offense*." Schelling's essay eloquently states the proposition that we do not yet know the true potential of nonviolence: "In the end it could be as important as nuclear fission." And, like nuclear fission, it has implications for all aspects of conflict and politics, none of which is yet easy to assess.

THE SCOPE OF REMAINING QUESTIONS

In the final chapter of this book the arena where ideas clash is widened and the counterpoint of detailed argument is sharpened. Margaret Fisher's "Contrasting Approaches to Conflict" is designed to leave the reader with a clearer view of the scope of conflict studies. She gives attention to extremes in dealing with the formulations of ethics-centered and ethics-denying approaches to conflict as represented by Gandhian satyagraha and praxeological theory. She concludes by posing questions that arise in attempts to apply the insights underlying these differing approaches to some of the seemingly intractable problems of our day.

In canvassing the literature on conflict—violent and nonviolent—the striking conclusion is that so many basic questions remain to be answered. And some have yet to be asked: Is there a force other than violence that can be used not only as a defensive measure but also as a moderating offensive strategy? If so, how could such a force be employed, and with what result? What are the dynamics involved in a process of changing a conflict situation in such a way that a new integration emerges? What would constitute adequate leadership for the conduct of a new kind of conflict? What would constitute the principles upon which such action could proceed, and what is the nature of the philosophy that would inform it?[12] If some viable force that can challenge violence is to be realized, much is still to be done—especially because the thought, the methods, and the theories that lie behind such efforts are yet to be developed.

The value of institutions and of processes through which man has sought to settle intergroup and international conflict is in no way to be minimized. Indeed, it is essential to continue the study of institutional change and analyze the process of law, taking note of changes in the forms and conventions already institutionalized in legal procedures. The distinctions between the state and society remain important considerations, and the reasoning whereby law has triumphed over the caprice of man in the governing process continues to be recognized as a highlight in political theory. We must pursue efforts to shape and improve organizational structures within which most conflicts can be settled. Moreover, the recent attention directed toward nonviolence as a dynamic concept deserves continued study. But the question remains: Sweeping and profound though it may be, is all this adequate to resolve the modern predicament of man? We may well ask what we really do have with which to cope with conflict situations resulting from the failure of institutions to keep pace with the need for change. And, above all, what is to be done when conflict strains the bounds of convention and breaks through the systems of deterrence into "hot" confrontation? The question comes down to this: how are we to manage without violence?

It would seem that we cannot in fact do without violence, at least as a last resort. And violence has always been available to most men. There is little reason to expect that success in replacing or minimizing violence will come first through our ability to effect basic changes in human nature. This is not to say that we can afford to overlook the need to understand the human condition. Nevertheless, many students of war and peace and of society and the state often turn to this "human nature" consideration only to be caught and held by arguments suggesting that change has first to be made in man's nature itself.

I am here arguing that we must begin with man as he is and that we must concede the inevitability of conflict. Failure to make this concession may well lead to some of the errors made by pacifists, especially those of an earlier period. We may be a step ahead if we begin our study with the candid acknowledgment that there will always be conflict of interest: conflict between men and groups of men which, on a grand scale, is conflict between nations. And when we speak of beginning with man as he is, we would do well to keep in mind that conflict within the individual unit of society—within each man himself—is also inevitable. How can we use this psychological fact to stimulate solutions to the problem of conflict on other levels? Ernest Jones, in Chapter 7, makes an important contribution. But the student of politics has to use his own tools to attack what is, in essence, a political problem, as well as using the findings of others to stimulate his search for solutions to the problem of conflict. Among the ways he may do this is through the careful selection of an analogue. I shall return to a brief discussion of analogical exploration from the field of psychiatry after making a few other observations about what we can learn from human nature studies.

Man often engages in conflict for the very reason that antagonisms require, indeed demand, resolution. It is, then, the resolving of antagonism that serves an emergent need. In this way conflict may be viewed as an active, dynamic process resulting from antagonism as well as a process that tends to resolve that antagonism.[13] The assumption is that conflict promotes and expedites decision.[14] Once more the reasoning turns to the significant matter of rational choice. The reader will note that in many of the essays included here rational choice emerges conceptually as a function, whether the text is dealing with violence, nonviolence, or symbolic violence. To force change is to force choice. And force is the appropriate word to use when speaking of struggles that have broken out of conventional channels into the "hot" conflict of intensive confrontation.

On the level of intrapsychic conflict, choice is related to rational decision in another way. And this may be of special significance because practitioners of the resolution of intrapsychic conflict, beginning with Freud, have achieved their objectives with a minimum of violence. The Freudian technique effects changes that allow for rational, conscious choice, for the therapeutic aim is to uncover repression, replacing it by conscious confrontation of problems that allows for the acceptance or rejection of what was formerly simply repudiated. It is of great significance that theory and practice are so intimately related in the Freudian approach. Just as Freud's theory points out the need for a conscious choice, his technique provides the means whereby that choice can be made. Through this technique (which may, at times, temporarily enhance conflict) repression is disclosed as a mechanism for evading the solution of underlying painful conflict. As such a mechanism, repression is not the cause of conflict but the avoidance of resolving conflict by the only effective means—deliberate choice.

The political scientist touches upon intrapsychic and interpersonal conflict not only because they are part of the human nature considerations that characterize so much of political philosophy but also because in telling us something about the character and purpose of conflict itself, they illuminate aspects of the sources of power with which politics is centrally concerned.

The extension of self-awareness, whether it is conceived in Western psychological terms or is abstracted, for example, from the Gandhian technique of satyagraha, speaks directly to that part of conflict resolution which treats both of a method of inquiry and a means for extending areas of rationality. One psychologist has argued that increased self-awareness is the key to survival. "You cannot be easily manipulated," Ann Roe argues, "if you know more about yourself than the would-be manipulator does."[15] She was writing about the essentials of change as well as about defense and a constructive approach to evolutionary advance.

Awareness of the self and the relationship of such awareness to action on the field of interpersonal or intergroup conflict is elucidated in the chapters on symbolic violence. But here again, neither technique nor theory has been adequately developed.

The popular trend is to suppose that concern with the individual self is sufficient or that some singly directed projection of that concern is the sought-for function—as in religion, where the relationship remains highly personal even as it interrelates man with some supernatural being. Again, the history of man is replete with efforts to escape the true problem of conflict as it develops between and among men. The function of mysticism as employed by some is to deal with conflict by avoiding the rational choice. However much the mystical experience may seem to satisfy certain personal needs, the questions raised by a steady look at conflict cannot be answered either by simple resolve not to be violent or through exercising the option to separate oneself from the great company of men who make up society; every man is conditioned by the values of his place and time, and those values are introjected into the individual mind—a process that, among others, distinguishes man as a species. If, then, man is a social being, whatever he does has its influence, even if what the individual chooses to do is to remove himself from active participation in the conventions of society. On the other hand, the exercise of rationally determined influence constitutes a kind of power, the consideration of which must enter into any effort to design a technique of action or to develop a philosophy of conflict.

Another constellation of questions follows hard upon those just raised. What are the uses of the past? This is not only a question leading to the significant question of how we have come to be as we are. At what peril do we ignore what has gone before? This is not alone the caveat Santayana posed when he spoke of the dangers of failing to understand history with the consequence of being destined to repeat history's mistakes. For if new contributions are to be made, we must know what has already been done. There may well be danger in supposing that we are doing something new without realizing that the action we are taking has been taken before, with consequences that, were we to know them, we might wish to avoid. There is still merit in the observation that "A man who does not know what has been thought by those who have gone before him is sure to set an undue value upon his own ideas."[16]

On the positive side of this same consideration is the proposition that if we do understand what has already been tried in other times and in other places we may well gain something of great value. This can be illustrated by measuring commonly held beliefs and assumptions about the Gandhian technique of satyagraha against the serious study of what satyagraha indeed is and how it has functioned in the conduct and resolution of conflict on the field of action.

These references to history are not meant to bind us to another discipline. We need to turn from the historical record to analytic considerations and to concern ourselves with theoretical foundations. In constructing an adequate paradigm from which experiments in the active conduct of creative conflict could then proceed, we need above all to sustain a questioning approach. As one contemporary political theorist has put it, "Misanticipations can arise from conjectures never made."[17] Nevertheless, we can learn from the history of ideas that the great leaps in man's knowledge have often come from cross-fertilization between fields, from intellectual exploration in the realm of analogy, and from multiple frames of reference. Is there, perhaps, an analogue from which we could advance toward meeting the challenge of taking that great step in knowledge which would lead to theory tested by action as applied to the problem of conflict? I suggest that such an analogue may lie somewhere within the psychotherapeutic arts. For this is the one field where techniques of resolving conflict (intrapsychic conflict) have been developed which do not utilize violence. It is also a field where theory and practice are intimately related and where rational choice is made possible through maximizing self-awareness.

At this point the student of the social sciences may well find himself full of questions about the relationship of the historical method to behavioral studies. In the present context he may be reminded of Frederick Watkins' observation that

> the position of the historians of political thought is comparable to that of the psychiatrists in the field of psychology. Just as the psychiatrist must proceed from the fragmentary and deceptive verbalizations of his patient's conscious mind to the more complex levels of subconscious experience, so must his political confrere use the potentially misleading but indispensable statements of political theorists, whose awareness of political matters is uncommonly acute, as a clue to the less fully articulate experiences and reactions of ordinary men.

Watkins perceives some danger in the psychiatric method "with its heavy reliance on tact and intuitive insight," but his point is that in both fields—psychiatry and the history of political thought—"the results achieved by competent practitioners throw genuine light on the nature of genuine problems," and, as he goes on to observe, in the absence of more effective techniques for the handling of such problems, "the psychiatric method has perforce to be accepted as an indispensable resource of modern psychology." He asserts that the historical method "must occupy a position of like importance for all those who are interested in the problem of political thought."[18]

Watkins' argument is for mutual understanding between scholars using historical methods and those devoted to behavioral studies. He takes the corresponding example of psychology and psychiatry and, in doing so, makes a valuable contribution. But my own point of abstracting an analogue from psychiatry takes quite a different direction. Before coming directly to that point some reference might well be made to the distinguished contributions of other contemporary scholars.

The collaborative effort of a number of distinguished social scientists in the 1950s on an analysis intended to yield a tentative theory of action (and the subsequent work associated with their initial study), whatever its substantial merits, does not provide us with the kind of breakthrough that satisfies the need for a theory of conflict. Talcott Parsons and his colleagues[19] attempted a systematic analysis of the action or behavior of living organisms, presented a general basis for a theory of motivation in institutionalized roles, and dealt with major aspects of the differentiation and organization of personality. The relation of economic theory to the general theory of social systems commanded foremost attention. Parsons was later to write that "it should be possible to work out a classification of the 'ingredients' of power, which is parallel to the factors of production, and as output categories from the polity, of 'types of power' which are parallel to the shares of income in an economic model."[20] This approach to aspects of a theory of political power had considerable influence upon scholars throughout the 1960s.

The contributions of Harold Lasswell continue to stimulate thought about political power and action. Here again, the questions I have to raise are surely narrower in scope but perhaps more elusive. Because they are focused sharply upon consideration of real and active conflict they may have seemed to lie outside the scope of political theory. But I shall argue that theory and practice must be brought together (as was the case in the development of psychiatry), for theory alone readily becomes sterile ideology, and action, without theoretical underpinnings, may well be fruitless and often presents unpredictable dangers.

There is no difficulty in accepting Lasswell's statement that the "demand to coerce is the phenomenon with which we are most concerned as professional students of politics" or that this phenomenon is the "distinctive characteristic of the social value that we call power."[21] His *Psychopathology and Politics* did indeed perform, as Lasswell more recently observed, "a positive part in pointing toward the configurative study of man in context," and his undertaking, aimed at performing the staggering task of making the "theory of political personality explicit for each important observational standpoint," has substantial merit.[22] But these far-reaching efforts are only peripheral to the problem of developing alternatives for the active conduct of conflict. However dimly the design may be perceived at this writing, it becomes ever clearer that an adequate theory of conflict must be sought through grappling with the specific problem of developing those alternatives to violence—alternatives that could be subject to experiment in limited instances of real conflict.

A TENTATIVE FIRST STEP IN CONSTRUCTING A THEORY OF CONFLICT

At the outset it cannot be overemphasized that, in constructing a paradigm suggested by psychotherapeutic approaches, the behavior of men in groups is not to be likened to that of individual patients in consultation with a psychiatrist. The suggestion is clearly *not* based upon the idea of "group psychopathology." It is only misleading to speak of what is sometimes called a "sick society" (therefore) requiring "treatment." The dangers of reifying society in this way are evident in several of the turnings of political thought in the past. It is essential to guard against the entrapment leading to the contention that conflict can be constructively resolved through the manipulation of the behavior of individuals. Such contentions are familiar in totalitarian polities where participation and involvement are both forced and manipulated.

As a model, the psychotherapeutic method has value for us for one distinct reason alone: The psychiatric encounter provides simultaneously an instrument for revealing truth and a technique for resolving conflict. The specialist is working with states of instability that vary from those of extreme crisis to relatively more stable or chronic states of equilibrium and disequilibrium, characterized by well-established symptoms. (It is perhaps not well known that the more acute or critical the psychological conflict, the more amenable it is to change.) [23]

Among relevant points to be learned from psychiatry is that the mentally disturbed individual expresses his inner conflict in ways that disguise the true nature of that conflict at the unconscious level and that the unconscious self-deception represented by the signs and symptoms outwardly exhibited or consciously recognized persist more or less painfully because—however distressing they may be—the underlying truth remains even more painful. In looking more closely at the resolution of this type of conflict we may emerge with some hypotheses about resolving conflict on other levels. The practitioner of the art of healing does not take the moralist's position of saying to the patient that he, the patient, is full of deception whereas the physician, the one who engages in the therapeutic encounter, is full of candor. Rather, the effective approach is that of proceeding with all integrity and candor in such a way that both parties are enabled to engage in the search for truth, in this instance, about the patient's inner conflict. The "truth" is an unknown that has to be elucidated with patience and over a period of time. What the therapist knows and the patient does not yet know is that the patient's method of expressing the conflict is unnecessarily deceptive, destructive, and uncomfortable—that there are other ways of managing conflicts which are more constructive and which could eventually free the patient from his symptoms, as well as freeing energy for work and for other pursuits.

Such an approach is akin to satyagraha, which is both a method of inquiry and a technique for engaging with others in situations of conflict. In the instance of psychotherapy, the creative process involved is the revelation of the nature of the underlying forces that constitute the conflict to both the one who is disabled by conflict and the one who intervenes. The analogue suggested here derives from the interaction of the physician who intervenes and the patient who, so to speak, is the battleground for intrapsychic elements in conflict. The psychotherapist's task is to help resolve the conflict. Among the processes involved are those of engagement, elucidation, interpretation, and reinterpretation toward the end of effecting change. The one who intervenes does not beguile the one caught up in conflict by offering another set of beliefs intended to dispel his delusions. Rather, through the use of different insights and without necessarily knowing or being able to reveal the full truth to the one torn by intrapsychic conflict, the intervening figure is actively engaged in a way of working that sets in operation a process of communication. This different way of conducting conflict shifts the psychological equilibrium in the direction of a new integration.[24]

To suggest that an analogue may be found in the psychotherapeutic arts is not to say that a *method* has been found or that a simple analogy adequate to the problem of intergroup conflict can be drawn. Rather, it only points one direction in which the search could be conducted for an alternative to violence for the conduct of conflict. If a paradigm were to be fully developed and a technique of action constructed, one would then have made only a beginning. For method requires testing if pitfalls are to be avoided. This is one of the most important lessons of history: Theory and method are never enough. But if, in the poet's words, we are to "transcend the cycle" of uncreativity and discover the "powers that could be used" to design the "means to free the node," it is imperative that we do more than *act* in unthinking ways, however much our action might be prompted by a sense of moral indignation or inspired by other profound feelings. For we speak here of fashioning an instrument through which conflict can be delimited and irrational action controlled. This requires more than massive involvement or participation— though such involvement, upon occasion, may be appropriate, as it was during campaigns of Gandhian satyagraha.

To perceive what is necessary requires a high degree of rational control over feelings—control that can then allow for adequate inquiry and for the thought that must precede the deed. The individual who, in this way, goes on to act constructively may find (as have many Gandhians) a sense of becoming, a realization of self that makes the demanding tasks required not only tolerable but also attractive. First to be perceived is the nature of the process, and then the dimensions of a given problem can begin to be understood. All this requires the development of a vehicle for action which, at this writing, is yet to be devised.[25] Surely, for our day, we must go beyond the Gandhian technique —as no doubt Gandhi himself would have improved, developed, and adapted satyagraha had he been working on the contemporary scene. Meanwhile, it bears repeating that just as theory must be put to the test on a limited, experimental field of action, action without an adequate philosophy to inform it carries seeds of destruction potentially more dangerous than the problems that prompted it.

Unlike other issues that engage the political philosopher, conflict, in its essential meaning for mankind, has rarely been dealt with in a systematic way. Violence and even nonviolence have indeed occupied the attention of men throughout the ages. And if only through indirection, conflict can be found to lie at the heart of many devices, conventions, and concepts that man has used to weave his web of governing controls. But when governments are challenged and conventions decay, when threats or fears triumph over reason in the counsels of men, then violent conflict emerges as regrettable proof that in all his history man has not found it possible to fashion alternatives to violence for the conduct of conflict. It is hoped that the readings offered here will stimulate interest in taking up the challenge. Many of the questions have been raised; yet others may lie embedded in these essays and in the works which have inspired them.

Those who can must look, and looking, see,
must think, and thinking, do, and doing, be.[26]

NOTES

1. From "Theme and Variations," an unpublished poem by Frank MacIvor Conway, 1946.
2. In Hannah Arendt's stimulating article "Reflections on Violence," *Journal of International Affairs,* 23, no. 1 (1969), 21–22, she argues that power and violence are opposites. "Violence appears where power is in jeopardy, but left to its own course its end is the disappearance of power." The difficulty with her argument is that she does not make clear her definition of power.
3. For a penetrating analysis of classical theories on problems of conflict see Kenneth Waltz, *Man, the State, and War* (New York: Columbia University Press, 1959). See also Stanley Hoffman, "Rousseau on War and Peace," *American Political Science Review,* 57, no. 2 (June, 1963), 317–333. For an illuminating survey of classical positions on terror see E. V. Walter, "Theories of Terrorism and the Classical Tradition," in David Spitz (ed.), *Political Theory and Social Change* (New York: Atherton, 1957).
4. For an exposition of the "dialectical" nature of the Gandhian approach see Joan V. Bondurant, *Conquest of Violence: The Gandhian Philosophy of Conflict,* rev. ed. (Berkeley: University of California Press, 1969), chap. 6.
5. "Reflections on Violence," pp. 32–33.
6. For a suggestive article on the relationship of "policy ends" and "policy means" in international relations, see Roland J. Yalem, "The 'Theory of Ends' of Arnold Wolfers," *Journal of Conflict Resolution,* 4, no. 4 (December 1960), 421–425.
7. David Spitz has reminded us that "democracy, alone of the forms of state, provides the necessary mechanism for its own correction." See his *Patterns of Anti-Democratic Thought: An Analysis and a Criticism, with Special Reference to the American Political Mind in Recent Times,* rev. ed. (New York: Free Press, 1965).
8. The many valuable works of Robert Pickus on civil disobedience are recommended to those who would read further. In his "Civil Disobedience But Not Violence," *Dissent* (February 1968), 19–21, Pickus asserts that "the problem is insurrectionary violence (and the attempt to create a climate for insurrectionary violence) masquerading as civil disobedience." He goes on to place the responsibility for damaging the antiwar movement upon those "who hold the mask but do not in fact accept the morality or politics of insurrectionary violence. . . ." Civil disobedience, he argues, *"is* at the opposite pole from insurrectionary violence" and "those engaging in civil disobedience in this country are not attempting to avoid, deny, or overturn the law" (p. 19). They must accept the consequences laid down by the law, as did Socrates.
9. Robert Pickus has used a similar line of reasoning, arriving at the very different conclusion that civil disobedience can perform this function and that civil disobedience always rejects violence ("Civil Disobedience," p. 19).

10. For a wide-ranging and brilliant analysis of pluralism see John W. Chapman, "The Political Theory of Pluralism," in J. Roland Pennock and John W. Chapman (eds.), *Voluntary Associations* (Nomos XI), (New York: Atherton Press, 1969), pp. 87–118.

11. Readers who wish to pursue the arguments introduced here would do well to consult Walter's, *Terror and Resistance: A Study of Political Violence* (New York: Oxford University Press, 1969).

12. See Portia Bell Hume and Joan V. Bondurant, "The Significance of Unasked Questions in the Study of Conflict," *Inquiry* (University of Oslo), (Fall, 1964), 318–327.

13. I am indebted to the work of Kurt Singer for the several ideas expressed here about the function and meaning of conflict. See especially his "The Meaning of Conflict," *Australasian Journal of Philosophy*, 27 (December 1949).

14. The sociologist Georg Simmel has suggested that actual struggle can be viewed as a form of solving conflict rather than as an instance of conflict. Some observers have called attention to an integrating function of conflict and have pointed to the fact that fighting requires a form of association. See the discussion of Simmel's position in the concluding chapter by Margaret W. Fisher, p. 192.

15. See Ann Roe's article, "Man's Forgotten Weapon," *American Psychologist*, 14 (1959), 262.

16. M. Pattison in his *Memoirs* (p. 78) as quoted by Lord Acton in William H. McNeil (ed), *Essays in the Liberal Interpretation of History* (Chicago: Phoenix Books, 1967), p. 306, n. 15.

17. John W. Chapman, "Political Theory," p. 105. In his argument relating to the comparative study of pluralism in modernizing nations, he observes: "If pluralism should become a style of thought, even as it accurately reflected trends in mature and industrialized societies, its diagnostic and predictive reliability could decline elsewhere." *(loc. cit.)*

18. Frederick M. Watkins, "Political Theory as a Datum of Political Science," in Roland Young (ed.), *Approaches to the Study of Politics* (Evanston: Northwestern University Press, 1958), pp. 154–155.

19. See Talcott Parsons and Edward A. Shils (eds.), *Toward a General Theory of Action* (Cambridge, Mass.: Harvard University Press, 1954). For a summary of that work, together with reflective comments, see Talcott Parsons, "Some Highlights of the General Theory of Action," in Roland Young (ed), *Approaches to the Study of Politics* (Evanston: Northwestern University Press, 1958), pp. 282–301.

20. Talcott Parsons, "Some Highlights of the General Theory of Action," in Roland Young, *Approaches*, p. 298.

21. Harold D. Lasswell, *Psychopathology and Politics, with Afterthoughts by the Author* (New York: Viking Press, 1960), p. 278.

22. *Ibid.*, p. 291.

23. In this discussion I am referring to the Freudian method as modified by developments stemming especially from ego psychology. It is of special interest to note that Heinz Hartmann, the distinguished authority on ego psychology, opened his essay "On Rational and Irrational Action" with a statement concerning an

analytical theory of action. "Since its beginnings," he wrote, "psycho-analysis has made important contributions to the psychology of action that clearly reflect the consecutive levels of analytic experience and thought. The approach became more explicit once a solid foundation was laid in analytic ego theory." Hartmann went on to say that there was not, as yet, a systematic presentation of an analytical theory of action but that, in his paper, he would "deal with a number of topics that would be parts of such a general theory." His essay is a stimulating discussion of the ends-means nexus in a psychological frame of reference. It was first published in Geza Roheim (ed.), *Psychoanalysis and the Social Sciences* (New York: International Universities Press, 1947), vol. 1, pp. 359–392, and was later included, in a slightly revised version, in Heinz Hartmann, *Essays on Ego Psychology: Selected Problems in Psychoanalytic Theory* (New York: International Universities Press, 1964), pp. 37–68.

For another psychological model in which, *inter alia,* psychology is recognized as "in large part a study of the internalization of society and of culture within the individual human actor," see Edward C. Tolman, "A Psychological Model," in Parsons and Shils (eds.), *Toward a General Theory*. It is perhaps worthy of note that this later work on a "general theory of action" does not make reference to the (earlier) statement by Hartmann.

24. For other analogical approaches see Joan V. Bondurant, "Para-guerrilla Strategy: A New Concept in Arms Control," *Journal of Conflict Resolution,* VII, no. 3 (September 1963), 235–245, and *Journal of Arms Control,* I, no. 4 (October 1963), 329–339.

25. For a suggestion about the development of a specific vehicle for action see Bondurant, "Paraguerilla Strategy."

26. Conway, "Theme and Variations."

I Familiar Modes of Nonviolence

1 *The New Peace Movement*

ROY FINCH

In this article Roy Finch reviews the history of "peace
societies" in the United States and Europe from their
founding in the early nineteenth century. We join his
discussion at the point where he introduces the forma-
tion of the Committee for Non-Violent Revolution in
1946. "In prison other pacifists engaged in work stop-
pages and hunger strikes," he writes. "Nonviolent resistance came to have a militant meaning, arising out
of the conflict with the government and the 'buffers'
of the historic peace churches."—Ed.

Such militant nonviolent action, however, gave rise
to new problems. How, after all, did nonviolent resistance differ
from violent resistance? Was not nonviolence just as potentially
coercive as violence? Could it not be used for just as destructive
purposes? In the attempt to answer these questions pacifists
turned to Gandhi. Gandhi had laid down the conditions for non-

From *Dissent,* 10 (1963), 86–93; 138–148. Reprinted (abridged) by permission
of the author and publisher.

violent action: that it must be undertaken only as a last resort, that it must be carried through without hate, that it must be aimed at policies and not persons. Such action was an attempt to use moral force as a weapon; it aimed at confronting opponents with the overt implications of their compliance with a social evil.

To be successful nonviolence had to be a matter of principle and not merely a technique; it had to be adhered to even under the most extreme provocation. It implied a degree of self-control which, even Gandhi admitted, could only be expected from a few. The majority might accept it only out of necessity. What was essential, in Gandhi's view, was that the leadership be committed to the principle.

The wartime resistance movements, particularly in Norway and Denmark where pacifists participated in the underground, raised the most serious problems. Gandhi had stressed openness and honesty. Under what circumstances, if at all, were secrecy and deception permissible? Could pacifists engage in the destruction of property, the blowing up of bridges and so forth, if there were no injury to human life involved? Could they forge papers, take assumed names, steal documents, cooperate with other underground groups engaged in killing?

The shift from nonresistance to nonviolent resistance brought pacifism into relation with traditional radical groups. Pacifists could now maintain that radicals had never been radical enough about their *means,* but only about their ends. Nonviolent action could be understood as the most advanced way of carrying on social conflict. It could be understood to include the actions of labor and minority groups when they went outside of established channels by engaging in strikes, sit-downs, demonstrations, and the like. The fact that the nonviolent aspect was often more a matter of necessity than of principle was regarded as an unfortunate weakness.

The nonviolent action point of view led also to the conclusion that revolutions failed because of their violence, which restored old power methods and built up a new fund of resentment and hatred. By copying the very methods of those they sought to overthrow, revolutions guaranteed their own failure. Violence, for the pacifist, is intrinsically reactionary, no matter who uses it or for what end. It is a pacifist dogma that "the more violence the less revolution."

Large-scale mass nonviolent action requires organization, training, and discipline, which are not congenial to the pacifist. Opposing authority, often at considerable risk, he submits unwillingly to another authority. Various proposals for a nonviolent army tend to run afoul of this strong antiauthoritarianism. Preserving spontaneity and informality and still keeping the discipline of nonviolence presents difficulties which pacifists are far from having solved.

Nineteenth-century radicalism had at its center a core of terrorism. The acceptance of this terrorism by Communists is vividly expressed in Trotsky's book of 1920, *Terrorism and Communism*. Trotsky wrote: "The terror of Tsarism was directed against the proletariat. The gendarmerie of Tsarism throttled the workers who were fighting for the Socialist order. Our Extraordinary Commissions shoot landlords, capitalists, and generals who are striving to restore the capitalist order. Do you grasp this—distinction? Yes? For us Communists it is quite sufficient."[1]

The Anarchist acceptance of terrorism is equally vividly shown in Alexander Berkman's *Prison Memoirs of an Anarchist*. Berkman describes the true revolutionist as one who is willing "to sacrifice all merely human feeling at the call of the People's Cause." Despite his contempt for it, the "merely human" keeps breaking through; it isn't so easy to be "superhuman." Berkman describes his attempted assassination of Henry Frick, the steel magnate, after the Homestead massacre. He has just shot and then stabbed Frick:

> An officer pulls my head back by the hair, and my eyes meet Frick's. He stands in front of me, supported by several men. His face is ashen grey; the black beard streaked with red, and blood is oozing from his neck. For an instant a strange feeling, as of shame, comes over me; but the next moment I am filled with anger at the sentiment, so unworthy of a revolutionist. With defiant hatred I look him full in the face.[2]

Here is the text for the anarchist—and the pacifist. Hatred is the antidote for shame. Having felt the "bond of suffering" which reduces everything to the "merely human," Berkman can only counteract it by invoking his hatred. Frick has to be transformed from a suffering human being into a class enemy.

Such "dehumanizing" of the enemy is the quintessence of twentieth-century ideology. A social grouping of class, race, or nation is given priority over the "merely human." An absolute enemy, then, in the absence of any principle of common humanity, is fit only for extermination. What the nineteenth century called "abstract humanism" is replaced by *unlimited social conflict justifying unlimited inhumanity*. Behind Berkman's contemptuous dismissal of the "merely human" lurk the coming shadows of Hitler, Stalin, and Eichmann. They all reflect the belief that some social grouping is prior to the human (a priority which unfortunately is embodied in the very word *social*-ism).

The terrorist aspires to be more-than-human, while his enemy, in his eyes, sinks to the less-than-human. The direct action pacifist, in his apoliticalism and extremism, has surprisingly much in common with the terrorist, but he refuses to be either more or less than human. He refuses to dehumanize either himself or his enemy. He does not regard "being human" as the easiest thing in the world, so that all our efforts must be bent on trying *not* to be human. On the contrary, it seems to him that "being human" is not something to be postponed.

To Trotsky's question: "The previous regime shot workers; we shoot capitalists—do you see the distinction?" the pacifist replies: "No, we do not see the distinction. A social or economic role does not qualify a person for being shot. And there is no blank check for doing the shooting. History does not make us either more or less than human. It does not relieve us of that much responsibility. We are not impressed by the ability or the need to disregard human feelings. That ceases to awe us. We have seen too many supermen now, and we do not trust them, especially when they have guns in their hands. Furthermore, we do not see history mysteriously turning murder into a good. We see only murderer and murdered reflecting each other and changing into each other again and again. Violence for us is not the measure of 'realism,' but of another kind of unrealism."

As indeed the Marxist understands, the proletariat have accumulated a moral capital which provides, so to speak, a temporary moral immunity for those who act for it, or even claim to act for it. But this moral capital is not inexhaustible. History, in the almost mathematical exactness of its retribution, permits only so much abuse of force. Marxism is not exempt from morality. It is based on a disguised moral passion, and without this moral passion it would vanish.

A more realistic view of human history cannot discount the role of human choice and hence of the moral factor. (What is the Khrushchev charge against Stalin, if not that he made wrong choices?) Besides every kind of necessity, there is, inescapably, human decision. And a third factor is also present—the factor of chance, the extraneous element which intervenes. History involves the complex interaction of all three factors—the ancient triumvirate of necessity, human choice, and chance (or fate, freedom, and fortune, the last replaced by Providence in the religious view). We cannot understand what happens or why things almost never turn out the way we expect or plan for, unless we take all three into account. The full concreteness of history lies in the interweaving of these three aspects, and leaving any one of them out distorts our understanding.

Under the influence of early modern science and its excessive causalism and determinism, social theory, including Marxism, tended to discount human choice and also the factor of chance (the latter perhaps present in human life as "spontaneity"). But necessity has a limited role, and there is no possibility of merely living in terms of that even if we wanted to. About this—that choice is always with us—we have no choice. The slow recognition that the moral factor cannot be expunged is being bought now at terrible cost. Scientifically, technically, there is nothing to be said against Buchenwald. It is only in moral terms that it can be condemned. To understand the *objective* nature of morality, however, will require a vast upheaval of thought, which has scarcely begun.

The radical's chief delusion has been the cabbalistic notion that he can "use" evil. He accepts this "filthy necessity" (the delusory "necessity" hiding the genuine moral "filth"), if not with a clear conscience, then at least with a secret sense of superiority, which in itself should have made his course suspect. He believes that he has been admitted into the arcanum of history, siding with the powers of good, and that now he knows that evil too can be of "use." But he deceives himself. He mistakes the Prince of Darkness for a scullery maid.

It is idle to talk about "humanistic radicalism" as long as we use the words "revolutionary necessity" to justify crimes—crimes which then go on and on. The use of executions, fear, terror, and lies as conscious policy under the pretext of "necessity" perpetuates the delusion that social progress can be made without any corresponding progress in the human and the humane. It is typical of this way of thinking that it efficiently describes this sacrifice of the human as the "human cost," as if human beings were what is expendable and the institutional framework and future goals were what really matter. The relativity of human choice, which is always with us, should not hide the difference between supporting human values in the present and being prepared to sacrifice them wholesale for imagined future goods.

The battle of the social engineers of various stripes (socialist, communist, capitalist) to tame the most intractable of animals —the human being—and compress him into suitable social molds is succeeding all too well today, but for reasons which escape the intelligentsia, who are usually on the side of the engineers and not of the human beings. The argument is most often about what molds and who is going to do the compressing rather than about how to escape this eventuality altogether. In this area fatalism runs rampant. We seem to know no answer but more and more social rationalization. It is a dream of total control, ostensibly aimed at liberating the rebellious human being but actually moving toward squashing every bit of rebelliousness out of him.

In this situation the pacifist, when insisting that human beings must be dealt with in human terms, that the human being is more important than any theory, and that the inhuman methods cannot achieve human goals, is pointing in the right direction. To find a new basis for political life and for carrying on social struggles is essential for a new radicalism. It is difficult to imagine what else can prevent further repetitions of the atrocities which go with twentieth-century ideological and nationalistic madness.

As nuclear energy and rockets are again revealing, science itself is intrinsically more revolutionary than any ideology or political or social movement. Merely trying to adjust to new scientific and technological discoveries imposes a perpetual revolution on modern societies. (Consider, for example, what social and economic effects would arise from discoveries—by no means impossible—of ways to synthesize food cheaply, manufacture gold in the laboratory, or change human skin pigmentation.)

Nowhere is the revolutionary character of science more evident than with regard to war. War has proved one of the most resilient of all human behaviors, adaptable to an endless variety of conditions and times. It has been able to incorporate new discoveries and still continue to be what it has always been—the final word, the extreme limit of communication, the ultimate "decision process." War has spelled human affairs in two words, "victory" or "defeat," but in this language it seldom failed to give an answer. Few human institutions or traditions have been so reliable.

Now, one is tempted to say, science is spoiling all that. For science is too literal, in a way too childish. It overdoes everything; it gives us more than we bargained for. War has a ritual character. It depends upon a fundamental rule of combat: that force will be sufficiently limited so that superior force may be rewarded. Force, in other words, must be kept within the limits which permit meaningful superiority if it is to serve military purposes. Overkill—that is, the ability to kill each person on the other side several times over—is not meaningful superiority. When the general "ground level" of force rises so high that superiority only appears in this region, then force no longer meets the conditions of combat.

Theoretically, victory in war might be determined by how many times over each side could exterminate the other, but actually people can only be killed once, and this sets a kind of "force ceiling." The military find themselves squeezed between the rising "floor" and this "ceiling" with less and less room to maneuver in. The enormous ingenuity spent on trying to make war still feasible within this shrunken space—that is, on exploiting other possible determinants of superiority—is an eloquent testimony to how reluctant we are to recognize the scientifically created dilemma of a world too small and a force too great for successful all-out wars. (The forces of modern science are actually sized for "space wars"—wars in outer space—and this may be a possibility. The orbiting of nuclear weapons would be the first step in that direction.)

The development of nuclear weapons has created a new spectrum in the peace movement. This spectrum now stretches from "nuclear pacifists" at one end to "unilateralists" at the other. Nuclear pacifists are primarily opposed to nuclear weapons, rather than to war in general, while unilateralists (comprising most traditional pacifists) favor varying degrees of American-initiated disarmament, regardless of what the other side does. Within these two groups and between them are a whole range of different positions. There is also a considerable overlap, since many unilateralists (borrowing a leaf from left-wing "front" methods, but without any subterfuge about it) are also active in nuclear pacifist groups and sometimes have even helped to form them.

Nuclear pacifists merge with, and share much of the general orientation of, the liberal-labor left. These are the "cause" people, those for whom a "moral" stance and a somehow "progressive" outlook are the essence of politics.

If peace has an international appeal, there should be an independent nongovernmental peace cause in the Soviet world. But where is the above-the-battle peace group in Russia? The American peace movement has rejected the alternative of working with government-controlled Soviet "peace" groups, correctly pointing out that the Soviet government is no more "peaceful" than other governments. That peace itself is not a weapon is precisely what has to be demonstrated. In the current sociological jargon the "peace game," if it is to be successful, has to be *completely* disentangled from the "war game."

At the other end of the spectrum from the nuclear pacifists are the unilateralists, including both those who favor unilateral nuclear disarmament and those who want general unilateral disarmament. This position is taken in varying degrees by most of the members of the older pacifist organizations, such as the Fellowship of Reconciliation and the War Resisters League, as well as members of such newer groups as Peacemakers and the Committee for Non-Violent Action.

The unilateralist point of view might be summed up somewhat in this way: In the release of nuclear energy science has made a technological breakthrough which must be matched by an equivalent breakthrough in human affairs. As even the military themselves recognize,[3] nuclear weapons are a *reductio ad absurdum* of war. But because of the inertia of old ways and the failure to grasp just how new the situation is, unless some absolutely new step is taken, these weapons are bound to be used eventually with immeasurable destruction and no "victory" for either side. Time is running out, and in the meantime the arms race continues. The only way to stop the doomsday trend is for one side or the other to take drastic action by announcing that it will start to cut back its weapons and actually taking the first step. The risk that the other side would take advantage of this would be great, but no greater than the risks of nuclear war, and the side which could really do this would gain an incalculable psychological and moral advantage. In fact, by giving up the Cold War it might actually "win" the Cold War.

Most unilateralists tend to agree that such unilateral action should be "phased"—that is, it should be done by the kind of steps which at each point would provide the maximum opportunity and bring the maximum pressure to bear on the other side to follow suit. The aim is not to tempt the other side all at once into aggressive action, but to provide the context within which it would be easiest for both sides to proceed in the same direction together. The *sine qua non,* however, is that the initial actions should be genuine, clear enough and decisive enough not to be mistaken for additional gambits in the Cold War. To the argument that if the United States acted this way, the Soviet armies at the first opportune moment would overrun Europe, there are two kinds of replies: the "reversible" unilateralist says that at some point it might be necessary to rearm, but at least the gamble for peace would have been tried, while the "irreversible" unilateralist maintains that we will have to learn to practice the only feasible method of conflict today—mass nonviolent underground resistance.

If all this is described as impractical and utopian, the unilateralist answer is that it is just what is "practical" that has failed and is leading us to destruction, and it is time now to try the "impractical." In an age when science has done the unprecedented, humanity will not survive unless it is prepared to do the unprecedented in other respects too. The absolute pacifist prescribes a dose of "impossiblism." He sees the issue of war, as the abolitionists saw the issue of slavery, primarily in human and moral terms. He refuses to forget the fact, obscured by strategy, gamesmanship, the Rand Corporation, and social scientists, that war is first and last an evil, bringing with it every human suffering. He reacts to this as a human being rather than as a computing machine calculating "acceptable casualty levels." The pivotal evil today, the place where all other evils focus, he declares to be war, and whatever must be done to get rid of war must be done.

Absolute pacifists have concentrated, not on political activity, but on direct action. Dramatic protests have been carried out, such as the voyage of the ship *Golden Rule* into the bomb test area in the Pacific, a walk from San Francisco to Moscow and a series of on-the-spot actions against Polaris submarine launchings. These actions are "gestures of conscience," signals in another language, crackpot only as all prophetic actions are. They make up for the smallness of the numbers involved by the extremity of the action. The absolute pacifist is more interested, in these times, in being "prophetic" than in being "progressive."

A number of different kinds of group direct actions have been developed, which may be roughly classified as follows: (1) picketing; (2) walks—a Gandhian method which has involved thousands; (3) vigils and fasts—a version of picketing, usually carried out by smaller numbers, sometimes in remoter places or over longer periods of time; (4) sit-downs—inside or outside buildings, at entrances to atomic plants or rocket sites, or, occasionally, in public squares, and sometimes coupled with (5) trespassings—on military installations, submarines, or government projects; (6) refusal to take cover in air-raid drills—carried out in several cities with growing numbers for many years now; (7) refusal to pay income taxes for war—another growing form of protest which often, however, leads only to the government attaching bank accounts or personal property.[4]

The important dividing line in these protests is between "legal" and "illegal" or civil obedience and civil disobedience. Confusion sometimes develops because of lack of understanding ahead of time as to just which is involved, though the same project may be planned to have both aspects, some participants cooperating with the law (for example, desisting when told to desist) and others refusing to cooperate (for example, "going limp").[5]

Since few people are converted by these actions and the public is likely to be either antagonized or indifferent, what purpose do they serve? The pacifist view is that they are a preparation for a time when peace sentiment will be widespread enough to make mass action possible and effective. In the civil rights field of the Negro struggle, the pacifist points out, similar actions were carried on for many years (often by some of the same people), and they are only now producing results. In the peace field eventually the same thing will happen, with even more revolutionary implications. "Do this long enough, and eventually it will catch on," one pacifist observes.

While some pacifists oppose political action on the grounds that nothing should be done to support the state since the nation–state itself is one of the chief causes of war, if it is not, in fact, synonymous with war, a much larger number have poured an increasing amount of energy into political campaigns.

There is a more deep-seated factor which comes closer to the real dilemma of the peace movement. That is that people do not trust peace candidates. They suspect them of being defeatist or of being willing to sell out to totalitarianism. The public image of the peace advocate or pacifist is likely to be of a well-meaning idealist who can easily be taken advantage of by less scrupulous enemies of freedom. Pacifism is equated with weakness and with less, rather than more, attachment to human freedom. (And it must be admitted that the behavior of pacifists themselves sometimes contributes to these stereotypes.) The basic problem is that military force is still the most convincing symbol and measure of a people's commitment to its tradition and ways (that is, the means by which people show how much they believe in what they do believe in), and pacifists have not succeeded in projecting some other symbol and measure.[6]

The most striking fact about the peace movement (even in its political manifestations) is that it is apolitical. This embraces everything from the sentimentalism which finds a positive virtue in not caring about politics (believing that good intentions ought to be enough for everything) to a conscious and intelligent rejection of politics on the grounds that abolishing war requires revolutionary change. In between are all those who make no special effort to bridge the gap between ideas which seem self-evident to them and the kinds of objections which are raised by ordinary Americans. The peace movement is not only politically immature; it has a "know nothing" quality which, besides limiting its effectiveness, would also make it fair game for political exploitation if the right combination of circumstances came along. A large number of people ready to support any program if only it is for peace—this almost invites political manipulation.

Many peace supporters, and especially young people, are apolitical for the reason that they are fed up with ideologies and ideological squabbling. They would like to forget all that. They feel that the fundamental human necessities ought to be simpler than that, and in one sense they are right. But the idea (implicit in so much peace activity) that all that is needed is to "get out and demonstrate" and experience an emotional togetherness, a folk-songy oneness, is a delusion. This is the atmosphere of cultism, of substituting automatic action and emotion for thought and communication. Action has its place, but not as an unconscious reaction. And, instead of longing for the short cut of mass emotions, the peace movement should devote itself to working out plans which make sense and a program which can be translated into the consciousness of ordinary people.

Peace as such is not a program; it can be coupled with many different views or none at all. And the word "revolution" by itself is not a program. And adding the two words "peace" and "revolution" together does not make a program. Pacifists who talk about revolutionary change may be forgiven for some vagueness, but theirs is a vagueness which extends even to fundamental principles. The enthusiasm of many leading pacifists for Castro, even after it was apparent that Castro had embarked on a one-party system and a dictatorship, showed that pacifists are not immune to the lure of the mass leader. But it also showed a fundamental confusion about pacifism and democratic principles. (Some of these pacifists had stated repeatedly in the past that they were opposed to *all* dictators, but this did not stop them from adjusting their principles to make an exception for Castro.) It wasn't until Castro went over openly to the Soviet camp—thus becoming an out-and-out participant in the Cold War—that some of them withdrew their support. On paper these pacifists had preached a Gandhian revolution of nonviolence, decentralism, and antistatism. In the showdown, however, it appeared that this Gandhian revolution was for the future, while in the present, in some situations, they would support revolutions of violence, centralism, and statism.

The revolutionary enthusiasm and unanimity of Castroism satisfied many radical pacifists who could not look beyond this enthusiasm to the totalitarian implications of the course which Castro took. They refused to see that a political structure which *makes possible continuing opposition* is the only thing that matters in the long run, since revolutionary unanimity cannot be sustained, and after it dies nothing remains in the one-party state but the enforced unanimity of the police. (There is an inevitable line where spontaneous support turns into coerced obedience, but this line is never visible in the totalitarian state.) The revolution which fails to understand the nature of freedom (which is *always* freedom for opposition), cannot help but turn into tyranny. In this respect Castro has betrayed freedom, and no supposed benefits or necessities (or contrasts with the horrors of the previous regime) can excuse or compensate for this. What began as a revolution for freedom abandoned that goal and turned into a reaction against freedom.

The Castro episode also revealed that the Communist question still has the power to cause serious dissensions in the peace movement—not over the question of working with American Communists[7] but over the question of the basic nature of Communism. Like others, pacifists tend to divide into "soft" and "hard." In the one group are those who basically do not regard Communism as a threat. They believe in the good intentions of Communists, are optimistic about the future development of Communism, and are not concerned about the possibility of world domination. On the other hand are those who are pessimistic about Communism. They regard it as a threat to human freedom (but one which cannot be stopped by military means). Pacifism for them is part of the answer, the way to resist totalitarianism effectively by seizing a psychological and moral advantage.

What is the future of the peace movement? It depends on whether peace supporters can remain true to their principle of rejecting both American and Russian militarism equally to work for a dynamic third alternative. Any attempt to apologize for the military moves of either side weakens the peace cause. Pacifists cannot support a Castro who lines up in the Cold War (for whatever reasons) any more than they can support those who would use military means against him and then expect to be believed when they say they are against *all* militarism. The revolution that is needed now is the revolution against war and militarism and both power blocs. It is imperative that somewhere in the world there be those who see beyond the present world conflict to forms and ways of life that will be superior to both alternatives in the Cold War and who, without compromise, will stand for this vision of the future. Anything less than this, any temporizing for the sake of expediency or of immediate gains, is a betrayal of the peace tradition and of the most urgent need of humanity.

The peace movement's task is to demonstrate that disarmament and ending the Cold War must take priority over every other issue and to show what possible ways there are to reach these goals. It is not only a question of persistently (and ineffectively) appealing for public support, but of working out the ideas which will be convincing. Peace has to be projected as a genuine alternative and not left as an unknown quantity which may seem more uncertain (and more fearful) than the military patterns so long familiar. Pacifists often give the impression of being more attached to their own ideas about *how* peace is to be brought about than they are to peace itself. They forget that the main question is reversing the trend toward war and that it is much more important that this be done than that some particular pacifist thesis be vindicated.

We are in a limbo now between a bankrupt and suicidal militarism which refuses to die and the beginnings of the possibility of world peace. The peculiar numbness which has hung over things since the advent of nuclear weapons is a testimony to how much is at stake and the fearful possibility that war will go out in one last overwhelming paroxysm. It is as if we have been holding our breaths against the moment of the turning point which we know will be the most decisive mankind has ever taken. In the meantime a last frantic pyramiding of fear goes on, the attempt to get rid of fear by more fear. This pyramid, like some monstrous inner growth, stretches to the breaking point. There remains only a short time. For the first generation in human history peace alone spells survival.

N O T E S

1. Leon Trotsky, *The Defence of Terrorism (Terrorism and Communism)* (London: Labor Publishing Co., 1921), p. 56.
2. Alexander Berkman, *Prison Memoirs of an Anarchist* (New York: Mother Earth Publishing Co., 1912), pp. 8, 35.
3. Gen. Douglas MacArthur, when visiting the Philippine Islands in 1961, declared: "Global war has become a Frankenstein to destroy both sides. No longer is it a weapon of adventure—the short cut to international power. If you lose, you are annihilated. If you win, you stand only to lose. No longer does it possess even the chance of the winner of a duel. It contains now only the germs of double suicide." Ralph E. Lapp, *Kill and Overkill: The Strategy of Annihilation* (New York: Basic Books, 1962), p. 7.
4. This list does not include refusing to serve in the army or to make or transport arms, which are, of course, the *sine qua non* for the individual pacifist. To the list could be added a few more uncommon actions such as the boat trips to the bomb test areas and to Russia, hunger strikes, burning of draft cards (after World War II), etc.
5. Pacifists often make a point of "working with" the police. After charges that peace demonstrators were manhandled in Times Square, a representative of the New York Police Department sat in on a pacifist conference discussing the best ways to carry on demonstrations.
6. The space race—for all its extravagance and military overtones—is perhaps desirable to the extent that it provides a nonmilitary focus for competition.
7. The Communist's view of peace is that "Soviet bombs are for peace; American bombs are for war." There is as little room for American Communists or Communist sympathizers in the peace movement as there is for American Legionnaires, and for the same reason. Each can easily be identified by his refusal to condemn militarism as such, impartially, on both sides.

2 *The New Pacifism*

STEPHAN THERNSTROM

The New Pacifism has been called into being by advances in military technology. Our age of nuclear terror has given new force to the pacifist dogma that war is the supreme evil, to be avoided at all costs. If pacifism is to become a significant radical force, it would be well to give its credentials careful scrutiny. Pragmatic choice of nonviolent tactics in appropriate circumstances is one thing; espousal of the pacifist world-view quite another. My purpose here is to insist on this distinction and to argue that pacifism as a total vision of life is highly unsatisfactory.

1. At the very center of pacifism is a core of faith which resists rational analysis and evaluation. A probing discussion of the roots of pacifism inevitably drives the pacifist into a leap of faith his questioner is unable to take. This is most evident when a secular nonpacifist confronts a religious pacifist. It is equally true, if less obvious, when he opposes a pacifist whose point of depar-

From *Dissent,* 7 (1960), 373–376. Reprinted (abridged) by permission of the author and publisher.

ture is humanist. The gulf that divides their views of "human nature" is ordinarily so profound as to be unbridgeable.

Hume has shown us the inescapable gap between fact and
value, and we all recognize that ultimate value judgments involve
some leap of faith. But the pacifist, I believe, displays a curious
eagerness to leap into darkness at the earliest opportunity rather
than as a last resort. A longing for absolute solutions is integral
to the pacifist ethos. Consider the recurrent pacifist complaint
that every war has "failed" and that hence we must abandon war
as a method of solving disputes. The simplemindedness of this
line of reasoning is staggering.

2. Three crucial premises of pacifist argument demand closer
inspection. The first of these is the assumption that the principle
of consent is sufficient to explain the functioning of a complex
social order. Deceived by the rhetoric of liberal democracy, pacifists sometimes speak as if American society were based entirely
on the consent of its members, and blithely assume that the principle of consent can be extended into the arena of international
politics. Pacifism of this variety is an especially näive version of
Lockean liberalism, which nervously lifts its skirts at the mention
of social *power*. Society is viewed as one vast Quaker meeting, a
collection of sweetly reasonable atoms in which decisions emerge
not out of conflict but out of "harmonious interaction."

This bias toward atomistic individualism, this blindness to
power is a radical defect. The pacifist stance is that of the Prot-
estant evangelist. The object of action is to win souls, and all
souls are equally candidates for salvation. Whatever the problem
—a strike for union recognition, an international crisis over the
economic privileges of an imperial power, a civil war—the pacifist appeals to the "spark of the divine" which is in every *individual*. The pacifist mentality is slow to recognize that societies are
more than mere collections of souls and that social decisions are
shaped by forces other than individual will. Society is a structure
of power, and the distribution of social power is determined by
the clash of competing interest groups or classes. Social change
takes place when one of the competing parties is able to grasp
further power and wield it successfully.

An awareness of power relations is the prime ingredient necessary to construct what pacifism lacks—a social philosophy which locates discontented social groups which constitute a social base for a political movement. Michael Walzer's early essay on "The Politics of the New Negro" [*Dissent,* Summer 1960] reveals that not all Americans, not all Negroes, but certain Negroes in a specific social situation have acted as the driving force in the Negro student movement. As Niebuhr observes, "those who benefit from social injustice are less capable of understanding its real character than those who suffer from it."

3. An important segment of the pacifist movement—represented by [the late] A. J. Muste and some younger radical leaders like James Lawson—can be partially exempted from this charge. Conceding that power pervades society, pacifists of this persuasion fall back on the assumption that there is a qualitative difference between violence and other forms of social power. They embrace, to varying degrees, political pressure and legal coercion as techniques of struggle, but unreservedly condemn the use of physical force. It seems plausible to distinguish sharply between violence and other forms of power in a society which enjoys democratic political institutions. Where law comes clothed in the language of high moral purpose, it requires some hardheadedness to see that behind every law, however unanimous the consent of its subjects, stands the policeman's night stick. The very essence of law, indeed, is the exercise of social power (ultimately physical violence) in order to restrain recalcitrant individuals or groups. Let the pacifist struggling to win freedom for the Southern Negro ask himself whether or not the exercise of federal power on behalf of the Negro in recent years has materially aided his cause. An affirmative answer raises the question: has not the threat of violence been the ultimate sanction which has made federal power effective? There may be debate over the expediency of dispatching federal troups to Little Rock at a given time. But can it be doubted that the position of the Negro in, say, Mississippi would be much more dangerous if the *possibility* of Northern interference were removed? Bayonets alone will win no permanent victory for human rights, but in a desper-

ate crisis sometimes only bayonets can protect them. (This is not, of course, to reduce the delicate legal and moral fabric of a democratic society to organized terror.)

4. A third pacifist tenet is the doctrine that "ends and means are convertible." From this premise it follows that one can never successfully use "bad" means for "good" ends, for bad means can have only evil consequences.

This is an age in which much blood has been shed in pursuit of utopia, and pacifists deserve credit for their perception that violence tends to be self-perpetuating. But it is false to insist that lesser-evil calculations must never be made in politics. Principled political action is in fact impossible without a clear grasp of the distinction between tactics and ultimate objectives, between ends and means. The *impossibilisme* which denies this is perilous, for when it is shattered by the imperative need to act, all restraint is gone. The history of the American pacifist movement in the thirties provides abundant documentation of this point. Pacifists here were generally quick to see the Fascist menace, and some urged aggressive "preventive measures" of a nonmilitary character which might have severely hampered the dictators in the early years. But as the world moved closer and closer to war, pacifist fear of American involvement began to blot out the movement's moralistic internationalism. Foreign policy moved to the center of the American political stage, and pacifists felt increasingly compelled to take politically relevant *action* against "that warmonger" in the White House. Forced away from their lofty internationalism by the pressure of events, many American pacifists then plunged into ugly isolationism.

5. A word on pacifist "successes." The pacifist asserts the universal applicability of nonviolent methods as a substitute for war and revolution, and triumphantly cites such "evidence" as the Indian Liberation movement and the Southern sit-ins. Of how much real weight as evidence for the pacifist proposition are such instances? The history of each is too complicated to enter into here, but one point is clear to the nonpacifist. In each case, the conditions of the struggle and the nature of the antagonist were peculiarly well suited to nonviolent action.

It is quite possible that the circumstances of our age will make nonviolence increasingly suitable as a technique of mass action. The development of military technology has already proceeded to the point where the state frequently possesses such a monopoly of the means of violence as to make it impregnable to military assault from internal revolutionary forces. The frontier nickname for the Colt .45, "Old Equalizer," sums up the age of small arms warfare now dead. In a world of tanks and jet fighters, Gandhian methods of mass resistance may be the only effective means of opposing a regime in many cases. But the only test of this hypothesis is the pragmatic test.

The pacifist true believer scorns such tests. For him, peace is the over-arching, all-embracing good (the Peace that surpasseth understanding . . .). He is right to maintain that nuclear war is unthinkable. But large-scale military conflict with conventional weapons is improbable and dangerous, not unthinkable. More limited military conflicts will be unfortunate, but these are almost certain to recur again and again. The choice of violence is evil, but often a lesser evil. Peace is a value, but not the highest value. There will again be times of painful choice, times when the radical must choose not peace but freedom and equality.

3 Limits to the Moral Claim in Civil Disobedience

HARRY PROSCH

. . . Nonviolent civil disobedience as such is not
new, of course. In fact, it is at least as old as Socrates. We find (according to Plato's *Apology)* that Socrates at his trial reminded his
fellow citizens that when the Thirty ordered him to go to Salamis
to arrest Leon he did not comply. He simply went home. The
context makes it clear that his disobedience was, however, disobedience to what he considered the illegal actions of civil
officials, not to the laws.[1] From the *Crito* we gather that Socrates could not be convinced of the wisdom of disobeying laws—
even poor ones and even in the face of death.[2] When Gandhi
and his followers in our times practiced passive resistance on a
wide scale as a means for gaining India's independence they
were not practicing disobedience to laws so much as disobedi-

From *Ethics: An International Journal of Social, Political, and Legal Philosophy,* 75 (1965), 103–111. Copyright © 1965 by The University of Chicago.
Reprinted (slightly abridged) by permission of the publisher.

ence to foreign administrators whose legitimate authority was not commonly acknowledged in India.

But what has arisen in America has been nonviolent disobedience to laws—and not only to outright discriminatory laws but also to laws, such as the trespass law, which are not in themselves discriminatory but which may be used to buttress discriminatory laws and practices. Such disobedience invites, and even demands, our careful attention. The way in which it skitters along the border between moral persuasion and the use of force, between passivity and activity, and between respect for the rule of law and for something higher than the rule of law must intrigue the student of ethics. But the fact that many of its proponents seem to claim that it ought to be regarded as not only morally permissible but also, sometimes, even morally obligatory constitutes a pressing demand that we give it a serious analysis.

A moral claim cannot simply be ignored by supposedly fair-minded people. To ignore it would be to put their own supposed "fair-mindedness" into serious question—even in their own eyes. But, since civil disobedience is not a moral claim made only in words, but rather one made in actions, it demands analysis from everyone—whether fair-minded or not. We may stop our ears to mere words—or remain apathetic—and our silence does not necessarily constitute approval or disapproval. Our silence has neither squelched the claim nor granted it. But when the claim is made in action, our continued silence or apathy either strengthens or weakens the effectiveness of the claim, depending upon the situation. If the claim (the action) is being met with forceful opposition by the authorities or by others and we remain inactive, our very inactivity helps to stifle it out of existence. If, however, the claim (the action) is not being forcefully opposed, and we remain inactive, our inactivity helps to fortify its existence in the world. Thus, whoever has not been for the civil rights demonstrators may turn out, in fact, to have been against them, and whoever has not been against them may turn out, in fact, to have been for them. An attempted action is like a "thing" which must either become established in the world or not, depending upon the nature of other actions which are or are not taken, whereas a word is not like a "thing" in this way—except in its character as an action. It is possible, in other words, to oppose the actions of writing or of speaking certain words—that is, to deny freedom of speech or of the press. But it is also possible to allow these words to exist as "things"—that is, to allow an action to be taken which sets these words forth into the world—but still to ignore the claim which they are making to an object or to a further action but which they are not in themselves actually laying hold of. Nonviolent civil disobedience, being a claim expressed in actions, not merely in words, demands therefore a consideration of its claim because it demands a decision for or against itself.

The most attractive moral rationale for nonviolent civil disobedience seems to run something like this: Some laws, or some practices buttressed by some laws, are unjust or wrong, and, in simply doing what these laws say you should not do—that is, in simply placing your body where they forbid it to be placed—you are only asking those who presumably believe in the justice of these laws whether or not they really believe in it. You are not coercing them by violence or the threat of violence. You are merely putting to them a question. And so your own hands remain clean. You are prepared to submit to their violence if their answer is "Yes." But the trick is that you are asking them in such a way that they will have to reply. Do they believe in the rightness of these laws firmly enough to continue enforcing them upon people who keep coming back to be arrested or even beaten? They must either act or not act in the face of your challenge, and so they must return an answer.

The tactic you are using appears, on this view, to be a striking and very effective mode of moral persuasion. However, since the employment of arguments—rational, emotional, or some combination—is not involved at its point of action, your opponents are not likely to identify your effort as an attempt at moral persuasion. They must rather tend to regard it as a power move on your part. Therefore, even though your action is nonviolent, its first consequence must be to place you and your opponents in a state of war. For your opponents now have only the same sort of choice that an army has: that of allowing you to continue oc-

cupying the heights you have moved on to, or of applying force
—dynamic, active, violent force—to throw you back off them.
Your opponents cannot now uphold the laws which they value
without the use of such violence. And to fail to uphold them is to
capitulate to you—to allow you to win and so to allow their laws
to become inoperative—*de facto* null and void. You have therefore literally forced them out of the possibility of contending
with you in the nonviolent arenas of moral persuasion (of the argumentative type) and of political maneuvering.

In terms of its practical impact, therefore, your tactic is basically a military one rather than a morally persuasive one—or
even a political one. It is a contest of force, even though the only
force *you* may be resorting to is that of the inertia of your own
body. It could possibly also have a morally persuasive effect if
your opponents already half-suspected the moral righteousness
of their own laws (at least subconsciously) and if the hard decision you are forcing them to make should result in their uncov-
ering their more deeply held principles—and also, of course, if
their deeper principles should happen to be the same as yours. If
and when it is reasonable to suppose that all these conditions do
prevail, then, at such a time and place, nonviolent civil disobedience would, no doubt, be mutually recognized as a genuine
mode of moral persuasion and therefore also as justifiable. This
"if" and "when" are, however, rather formidable. The chance of
error in the assessment that these essential conditions do prevail
in some particular instance is great. . . .

It is true that the eventual outcome of the argumentative
forms of moral persuasion is also quite problematical. But the
penalties for failure in such argumentative attempts are not as
great as are the penalties for failure in this nonargumentative
form. If this form fails, one has succeeded only in increasing the
hostility of one's opponents toward one's views, and actually
therefore in creating a greater obstacle to the moral re-evalua-
tion one is ostensibly seeking. And then there is, in addition, the
further considerable risk that "nonviolence" may spill over into
"violence" when it meets with the counterviolence which it has
provoked if it has not been successful. This latter risk, in fact,

might almost be said to be a tendency. History seems to show us that it is very hard to keep limited wars limited—especially when one or more of the contending armies are popular armies who popularly think of their enemies as morally deficient. "Whosoever taketh the sword," Christ might have said, "shall be condemned to use it."

In view of all these uncertainties and dangers, nonviolent civil disobedience, thought of as a mode of moral persuasion, seems indeed to be a risky business. Not only are the chances of success not very good, due to the difficulty in knowing when the proper conditions for its success prevail, but the penalties for failure are rather severe.

When we note, therefore, that nonviolent civil disobedience seems to be widely used and respected as a form of high moral endeavor by those who are apparently not aware of its considerable risks, we should suspect there is something more to its moral rationale than its precarious usefulness as a means of moral persuasion. Why should one choose such a risky way to persuade? How can one morally justify this choice? If its only moral justification is its capacity to serve as an effective means of moral persuasion then it can be said to have little, if any. The moral rationale of nonviolent civil disobedience requires another principle able to justify it as an action regardless of its success or failure in moral persuasion. A principle fit to do this would then constitute its primary moral justification, and the additional fact that its nonviolent form also leaves the door even slightly ajar for moral persuasion would then merely add to its moral attractiveness, rather than, in supposedly defining its moral purpose, actually condemn it.

It is not too difficult to identify the principle that constitutes such a primary moral justification for nonviolent civil disobedience. Proponents of civil disobedience extol it in their songs and stories, their legends and their heroes. It is the simple and popular notion that it is morally right, and even heroic, to oppose unjust laws, to take a forceful stand in battle against them, and to overcome them, even at great sacrifice. This principle does, in fact, beckon to us all, because we all see to some extent that it is absurd to suppose that every law is *ipso facto* right—that no law can be subject to criticism. In fact, we all surely must be aware of some laws that we ourselves are critical of. But if laws, as such, can be subject to criticism then it naturally seems to us there must be something that is right in terms of which they can be criticized. This "something" must be then what is truly right, and laws which we are not able to square with it must be truly wrong. But even to follow or to act according to a wrong law is surely itself to do what is wrong. It must, therefore, seem right to us to disobey, to contend against, to try to overturn, in a word, to *fight* these wrong or unjust laws.

We therefore have to turn our inquiry into a more general one. We must investigate the moral adequacy of the principle common to any form of protest civil disobedience: It is right to use force in the attempt to nullify or to change unjust laws. Force is the most general term to use here, since, as we have seen, even nonviolent disobedience involves a resort to force, and it is the rightness of the use of such a means as this against unjust laws which is the crucial issue, inasmuch as it is this use that distinguishes disobedience from other peaceful (rule-abiding) modes of opposition.

Since the rightness of the use of force hinges, in terms of this principle, on an opposition to unjust laws only (anarchism or despotism—a total rejection of the rule of law—is not presumably what is being advocated), let us begin by inquiring into the criteria for correctly or rightly applying the term "unjust" to laws. Here we may profit from the work of the language analysts in philosophy. If we are asking for the criteria for the application of a word, we must, as many of them have pointed out, seek for the shared, common, or public way of applying the word—a way which does, in fact, communicate with those who are using the language. Otherwise we would merely be trying to speak a private language. . . .[3]

If this is true, our question then must be: Do we have a way of deciding in a public fashion what laws to designate (what laws we ought to designate) unjust? It turns out that we have at least two ways, sometimes involved in each other, for deciding this in a public way—and also for agreeing publicly that we have decided it rightly. One way is by the argumentative forms of moral persuasion. The other is through the operation of commonly accepted political processes. We are sometimes able to argue each other into an agreement that a certain law is unjust or wrong or bad and that it ought to be opposed. And we are sometimes able to accept a repudiation or change of a law which has been accomplished by what are publicly regarded as ordinary political processes—such as the repeal or modification of a law by a constitutionally legitimate legislative body or (in America) by a Supreme Court decision that a law is unconstitutional.

Neither of these two ways, however, can be what we seek, for although they are both public ways of designating laws as unjust, they are also, at the same time, public ways of changing such laws—and, moreover, changing them in peaceful or noncoercive ways. If we could have achieved a public designation in one or the other of these ways, we would not find ourselves involved in the use of force to accomplish a change in the laws.

So our question must be sharpened into whether or not, when we are trying to change or oppose laws by force, we have a public or common way available to us for identifying these laws as unjust. And it should be obvious from what has been said that we do not have and that we cannot have. Our not having such a way defines our situation. Where force is resorted to, some individuals think the laws under fire are just and others think they are unjust—that is, think the laws should be designated "unjust." It is quite clear that these two groups are not using the same criteria for the application of the word. As a matter of fact, they will still not agree on the criteria for its use even after one side wins. Such agreement is, by contrast, forthcoming from successful persuasion, and some sort of agreement arises from successful political action as well. We all do agree, for instance, that a law which has been repealed in a commonly accepted, legitimate manner is no longer a law that ought to be obeyed—in spite of the fact that many of us may not have been morally persuaded that it was a bad or unjust law. What we are morally persuaded of in common, in this case, however, is that the methods used in securing the political decision were right or "proper" ones. Our agreement on these methods is, in fact, what constitutes our political community. To the extent that such methods are lacking, either anarchy or despotism is present. But when the defeat has not been a moral or political one, but merely a physical one, there is no agreement—even upon the fact of defeat. Defeat is regarded as only a strategic withdrawal—the fight is still in progress. This appears to be the case for instance, in the American South—even after a hundred years.

A resort to force is, of course, thoroughly understandable when deep and serious disagreements exist and when neither moral persuasion nor political methods seem equal to their resolution. But it can hardly be said in any common, disinterested, or objective way to be morally right or just. What is morally right or just seems to remain as controversial after the use of the force as it was before or during it, and it would therefore be a strange (or possibly only an emotive) use of the term *moral* to apply it to a method for dealing with a moral controversy which can be seen analytically to be incapable of achieving a moral resolution.

But this conclusion meets with considerable resistance from those who find themselves in a serious moral disagreement with what the laws provide, such as in the case of the civil-rights controversy. It still seems to such contestants that the cause for which they are fighting is just and right and that to fail to fight for it would be wrong since it would be, in effect, to acquiesce in the wrong, namely, in what the laws now provide. Somewhere behind such a "feeling," therefore, must hover the notion that public agreement on the criteria for the use of such a word as "unjust" is irrelevant and unnecessary, that everyone has his own moral principles and standards, and that they are rendered neither more nor less right by being also in agreement with public criteria. Ethics must therefore be thought, however dimly, to admit somehow of private criteria for the application of its key words—or else it is thought that the whole enterprise is only emotive, that is, merely an elaborate conventional and ceremonial way of expressing our feelings (like saying "Ouch!" and "Yum! Yum!" only much more complicated). At least, since the contention that it is right to fight for the right (i.e., against the unjust) must, as we have seen, deny that public agreement is essential to labeling something unjust, it seems difficult to see what criteria other than these are left. Let us therefore examine our language more closely to see whether or not we are merely speaking a private language in ethics—or are merely using words emotively.

When someone says, "It is right to fight for the right," he could, on the view that public criteria for the use of his ethical words are inappropriate, mean (or express) nothing more than that he thinks (or feels) it is right to fight for the right. He could not mean that it is right in some public sense of the word, for then, in the end, he would be holding that some public sense of the word "right" is possible after all, and he would be thrown back into seeking for this sense and therefore into seeking for the ways of achieving public criteria for words like "right" or "just." These ways would have to be, as we have seen, argumentative persuasion and/or political maneuvering—not at all fighting. So he must not be understood to be stating something having a genuine public meaning when he says it is right to fight for the right. And yet, if someone did make such a statement as this, would he, in fact, be understood to be only asserting (or expressing) something of his own feelings? Would he not also, as Charles Stevenson suggested with respect to the moral use of the word "good," be understood to be inviting from others an agreement with him on his feelings?[4] Indeed, as this expression is in fact used, he might even be understood by his hearers to be demanding, or at least contending for, such an agreement. But whether or not we do actually contend, or demand, or only invite an agreement with us from others by the use of our moral words, it seems clear that to say something is (morally) right is not the same as to say it is appetitively delicious. . . . Men in real moral controversies understand quite well what is set forth by their opponents. To assert that something is right is to assert that everybody ought to permit it—if not to do it.

If this is what is involved in men's serious moral talk, it should follow that no principle could then be fit to serve as an ethical principle—as a principle operative in an ethical system of coherent rights and duties (moral obligations)—unless it is capable of becoming a common principle of action. Let us ask, therefore, whether the principle that it is morally right to fight for the right is one which is capable of becoming a common principle of action.

Since a fight, as such, necessarily entails crossing the will of others in a forceful way, the best hope for finding that fighting for the right is fit to be a common ethical principle lies in discovering some ends or causes that are rationally or intelligibly justifiable and so are *potentially* capable of becoming common. This was, as a matter of fact, how Kant was able to make his merely formal categorical imperative also a material one, useful in making distinctions between better and worse ways of life.[5] It might seem that if there are some causes which are really right as causes, then to fail to fight for them must really be wrong. But the difficulty is that, even if we are sure that we have our fingers on the really right ones, our opponents are also sure they have their fingers on the really right ones, too, and, as long as we have been unable to agree with each other upon which ends or causes are the truly right ones, the principle that we ought all to fight for the right ones would be far from providing us with a common principle to live by. It could only be said to be common to us in an abstract sense. Since we would be putting different concrete fillings in it (battling for different causes), it could only lead us in practice to tear each other apart in thoroughly unprincipled ways. And this would be true even if we tried to amend the principle to take care of this objection and said, for instance: "It is right for everyone to fight for whatever he really thinks is right." We would find this principle could only defeat itself in the sort of action where it should presumably come into play, namely, where there was something to fight for or against, where we did not all agree upon what was right or just—other than the principle that it was right for each of us to fight for what he thought was right. If we really tried to grant our opponents the right to fight us (which would be to grant them the power and the privilege of fighting us), we would not be truly engaging in what the principle said was right—a fight for the right. Either it is right to fight, or it is not. If it is then we ought to *fight,* and it would be wrong to give up or to lose the fight by restraining ourselves to some set of restrictive rules. If it is right to fight for the right, it is surely wrong to fail to fight in the way we find we have to fight in order to win. We could have no right, under this principle, to turn the fight into a mere contest and so risk failing to bring about the right. . . . So none of us could, in practice, actually follow such a principle. We would have to confess ourselves, therefore, as out of ethical relations altogether with our opponents in a fight for the right—we would have to admit that they would always have as much, and as little, reason to claim their actions were moral as we would. Being out of moral phase with each other, only God could be our judge, and the only morality our fight could have would be that of a medieval appeal to Heaven—a trial by arms. Most of us are no doubt sufficiently freed from superstition to recognize that in such a case it could only be the stronger who would win—or at most the more fortunate—not necessarily those who were more "right."

What this should mean to us is that we cannot moralize fighting. To restrain our fights by the principle of nonviolence is admirable as an indication of a yearning for righteousness on our part, a desire for a morality which we somehow divine does not lie wholly in our fight-for-the-right itself. And it would also transform the fight into an attempt at moral persuasion, were the conditions mentioned earlier in this essay to prevail in some particular instance. But it does not in itself moralize war. A fight, a state of war, is not and cannot be a moral state. Either we govern our relations by notions of mutual rights (i.e., ethically) or we govern them by force. There is nothing in between.

Yet there is no doubt that we will all still—in spite of the calm analytical facts of the case—fight for the right, "as God gives us to see the right," when the chips are down and the battle lines are drawn. What else indeed can we do? But it would be unintelligent to regard this fighting as anything more than a last resort when all else has failed—as a most regrettable and even tragic situation. We surely ought to restrain our primitive impulse to regard it as our supreme moment of truth—as a glorious and glamorous opportunity to flail about, cracking heads for a noble cause, filling our little lives with meaning in this manner, and accomplishing the will of God. A struggle for the "right" may at some time become a sober and solemn necessity, born of the circumstances and laid upon us in spite of ourselves. But then the only joy in it, meet and proper for us to take, should be something akin to the peace the Stoics found in resignation. A true fight for the right should be for us not really a fight at all, but rather a quest for a common ground—a patient and unromantic effort to be reasonable and tolerant, persuasive and conciliatory, in an attempt to reach decisions which may have in them little more than the commonplace virtue of being common—at least in the mundane political sense. Short of having made this supreme effort, we shall not—if our analysis here has been sound —have kept our hands clean, regardless of whether we wage the fight thrust upon us by violent or by nonviolent means.

NOTES

1. Plato, "Apology," *The Dialogues of Plato,* trans. B. Jowett, 2 vols. (New York: Random House, 1937), vol. I, p. 415.
2. *Ibid.,* pp. 434–438.
3. A good brief résumé and defense of the later Wittgenstein's views on the impossibility of a private language—even in terms of words like pain—is found in Norman Malcolm, "Wittgenstein's *Philosophical Investigations,*" *The Philosophy of Mind,* ed. V. C. Chappell (Englewood Cliffs, N. J.: Prentice-Hall, 1962). See also Norman Malcolm, "Knowledge of Other Minds," *ibid.,* esp. p. 152.
4. Charles L. Stevenson, *Ethics and Language* (New Haven: Yale University Press, 1944), pp. 25, 26.
5. Immanuel Kant, *The Fundamental Principles of the Metaphysics of Ethics,* trans. T. K. Abbott (New York: Longmans, Green, 1900), pp. 66–68; and Immanuel Kant, *The Metaphysical Principles of Virtue,* trans. James Ellington (Indianapolis: Bobbs-Merrill, 1964), pp. 42, 42, 46, 114, 126. Here Kant's language, especially on p. 126, might even be interpreted as providing at least a limited justification for precisely the kind of fights for the right which are now current. He says, "Therefore, reconcilation *(placabilitas)* is a duty of man, although it is not to be confused with the weak toleration of wrongs *(ignava injuriarum patientia)* which renounces stern *(rigorosa)* measures to forestall continued wrongs by others. For that would be to throw one's rights at the feet of others and to violate man's duty to himself." Kant does, however, reject revolution elsewhere.

4

The Moral Ground of Civil Disobedience

DARNELL RUCKER

Harry Prosch's article, "Limits to the Moral Claim in Civil Disobedience,"[1] confuses *civil* disobedience with defiance of law as such and consequently seems effectively to eliminate what has long stood as the last bastion of the individual against his society, short of open rebellion.

Prosch's reference to Socrates in the *Apology* is indicative of this confusion. True, Socrates' disobedience of the Thirty was disobedience to what he considered an illegal government—but it still was disobedience to the government in power, disobedience in the name of justice.[2] The disobedience *was* civil, since Socrates did not attack or otherwise try to overthrow the Thirty; he simply went home and expected to be put to death for his act. Even more instructive, however, as to Plato's views on civil diso-

From *Ethics: An International Journal of Social, Political, and Legal Philosophy*, 76 (1966), 142–145. Copyright © 1966 by The University of Chicago. Reprinted by permission of the publisher.

bedience is Socrates' announcement to the jury and the citizens of Athens that they need not order him to cease his activities as a philosopher because *he will not obey them* but will continue to obey the god.[3] Socrates here is not defying unlawful rulers but the duly constituted voice of the laws of Athens. As he points out in the *Crito,* the laws have no voice of their own; they can speak only through men, and whatever the jury decides becomes the legal decision.[4] There is no other source for determining what the law is or how it applies to particular cases.

The subtle distinction between Socrates' position in the *Apology* and in the *Crito* is precisely that between civil disobedience and defiance of law. Socrates in the *Apology* says, "I shall not change my conduct even if I am to die many times over."[5] He does not deny that the jury has the authority to command him to cease his search for truth if such is their interpretation of the law and of his profession. But he claims the prerogative of accepting their penalty (even of death) rather than their law. Having made this claim, Socrates is bound to submit to the sentence imposed upon him (whether justly or unjustly) by the jury. Hence, in the *Crito,* Socrates refuses to defy the laws of Athens by attempting to escape after he has been condemned to death.

Socrates did not consider himself as a destroyer of the laws when he said that he would not obey any order to desist from his philosophic activities. He openly stated that there were certain things that, as a man, he would not do; yet, as a citizen, he stood prepared to undergo execution if so ordered. Had he tried to evade his punishment once he was sentenced, he *would* have been a destroyer of the laws.

Men are, of necessity, social beings; they are not thereby automatically chattels of whatever sort of society they happen to find themselves in. Moral persuasion and orderly political processes are obviously the preferable means for a man to use to change those things he finds wrong in his society. But moral persuasion, to be effective, requires in those to be persuaded a special set of conditions which may be entirely beyond the control of the man attempting the persuasion. And use of the legal machinery for social change requires a certain amount of political power and a particular leverage in order to make that power felt in the right places. If the morally acceptable defenses of the individual citizen against laws he finds unacceptable are restricted to moral persuasion and legal processes, then the man who can find no audience and who has no power is left with no moral resource within the structure of the society, and his only recourse is violence—rebellion or crime. Moral persuasion is an empty phrase to the Negro in Mississippi who is effectively disenfranchised and virtually unprotected by the law. Orderly legal change is an impossibility for the man without a semblance of legal right or power.

Civil disobedience does present another moral alternative, fortunately. If a man finds a law morally unacceptable to him (and, of course, he may be justified or unjustified in his finding), he has a right to say to his government, "I will not obey this law, but I will accept the punishment connected with that disobedience. I will endure your penalty rather than commit an injustice." Law presents (or should present) us with a clear alternative: obey this law or suffer this penalty. As rational beings, we have a choice with respect to the law as well as an obligation to the structure of law. Changing or abolishing a law by legal or revolutionary means involves both a span of time and special conditions. In this immediate confrontation of a law, the citizen is within his rights to disobey openly and in full willingness to accept the penalty.[6]

Civil disobedience is ordinarily a last resort short of violent action. Civil disobedience is necessarily nonviolent; violence against the law and its officers of enforcement is rebellion or crime. The civil dissenter does not attempt to escape the punishment inflicted upon him. Neither does he claim extenuating circumstances in his case nor the legal invalidity of the law nor any other ground for the nonapplicability of the law to him or his act. Civil disobedience is not a matter of challenging the legality of a law or of ascertaining the meaning of a law.[7] It is a matter of a man rejecting a moral demand of his society at the same time that he admits the legal right of his society over him.

Men do require society, and society requires government. Government requires an ultimate sovereign power, a final legal authority such that once it has spoken there is no appeal beyond it except to heaven. Otherwise, as Hobbes has so forcefully pointed out, there would be no way for disputes ever to be settled peacefully. Human existence is possible only in societies, and human societies are formed by law, and law must have a sanctity in order for society to persist. But so long as the law is dealing with men as rational beings, it cannot command simply do this or do not do this; it must say do this or do not do this— or else. And the "or else" provides an essential alternative *within* the structure of law. The man who acts in defiance of law with the intent to escape both the command and the punishment is acting outside the law. The man who says "No" to the law's command and stands still for the law's "or else" is operating within the law.

Some may see this view as a basis for anarchy. Yet it contains the seeds of anarchy only for that society whose laws so ill fit the needs and desires of its people that they find it generally more desirable to undergo the penalties than to obey the laws. That society would already be anarchical in structure regardless of the basis for disobedience on the part of its citizens. States attain such stability as they have because the general structures of law of which they are composed do serve at least to a tolerable extent the needs of the communities they embody. Civil disobedience cannot rightly be called a military tactic since it is not directed at the destruction (violent or nonviolent) of law as such, nor does it offer any resistance to the officers of that law. The rebel and the anarchist aim at the overthrow of the state; the civil dissenter acts strictly in recognition of the law and its authority.

An act of civil disobedience cannot be justified on the uncertain ground that the agent has correctly read the mental, moral, and emotional condition of other people in his society so that he has reasonable assurance that his act will succeed in bringing about a change in those people such that they will change the law in question. That ground is so uncertain as to make justification practically impossible. The moral warrant for civil disobedience is not a successful moral psychoanalysis of anyone nor an accurate prediction of anyone's reaction to the violation of law. Rather, the justification rests on the individual agent's choice to submit to the coercive force of the law instead of acting against his interest or his conscience in accordance with the law.

How will a man know that he is serving his interests better by accepting the law's retaliation rather than its command? He will not know until after the fact, if at all. This is true of all action; we never act in prior certainty of the effectiveness of our action. In a well-ordered society, a reasonable man will usually think it to his advantage to act openly in obedience to law or covertly in disobedience. How will a man know that his conscience is right against the law of the land? He will not know, of course. No man ever *knows* that any moral judgment is right, but as a man he has to act on the basis of his moral judgments as his experience and intelligence enable him to make them. Here, too, in a well-ordered society, a reasonable man will be hesitant in asserting his judgment against that of his society. The preponderance of power will always be on the side of government, and the reasonable man will weigh the importance of the issue at stake against the probable consequences of his open disobedience of that government.

As an agent, a man retains the right to choose to disobey, however. The very concept of human society (and consequently the concept of law itself) rests upon the concept of rationality. Rational beings alone—beings capable of acting in accordance with the concept of self-given law—can constitute a society under law. Any political theory that maintains the absolute subjection of the individual to the political machinery within which he chances to exist cuts the ground from under political theory itself. If the beings who constitute a political community do not retain the right and ability to choose their own acts, the political community is inexplicable both as political and as a community.

The *legal* decision as to the justice or injustice of a law is always a public matter. The contention, however, that the individual's judgment as to the injustice of a law must be made as a public decision or evaporate into a mere state of mind reduces all morality to the crassest kind of political positivism. All judgments as to justice and injustice should be publicly *defensible,* and the man who makes the judgment should stand ready and willing to defend his judgment or to be dismissed as a crank or worse. There is no guarantee that anyone else will *listen* to such a defense, of course, or that those who do listen will be convinced. Any such requirement for a moral judgment reduces morality to an absurdity. Socrates was not wrong because he failed to sway a majority of the jury that tried him. He had little hope to begin with that he *could* convince that jury. Still, he saw his obligation to state his case as objectively as he could, to lay out his argument for any man to attack and to take account of any cogent attack forthcoming. His argument stood; the majority of the jury was unmoved by that argument. As a man, Socrates was responsible for his argument, publicly defended. As a man, he did not have power over (hence he did not have responsibility for) the reactions of his audience. Socrates did not make his case in terms of his private criteria of the good or of his emotional state with regard to the good. He made his case in terms of an argument, an argument that his public refused to accept but one that he had to stand by in the absence of any convincing counterargument.

A viable political society is one in which the regulations and enforcements instituted enable that society to function (whether well or limpingly) and in which law works primarily in the positive sense of providing an atmosphere of general expectation of compliance with law. But law cannot be such a positive force unless it is, at the same time, a negative, a coercive force. Law that works well works by providing for a community of action within that law; it must also work by threat of reprisal for action that breaks through the limits set by the law. The more effective a society is in providing for the growth and development of its citizens and their functions, the more nearly its laws work as positive guides for action. The less effective a society is in these regards, the more its laws have to work negatively by use of force against its citizens. Nonetheless, unless we are content to hold that law as law is right (whether it works well or badly and whether it provides orderly means for change or not), we must hold that the citizen retains his right to say to the law, "I will not obey though you kill me many times over."

This individual right cannot be restricted to the man who attains moral certainty in his disobedience. Only a god has moral certainty, and a god has no need of such a right. Men are peculiar beings who by necessity live under conditions such that they are at once parts—cogs, if you will—in a social machinery *and* persons whose highest responsibility is to themselves as moral, intelligent, and aesthetic beings. A theory that makes the individual supreme over all other considerations is a theory for anarchy and the destruction of man. Likewise, a theory that makes the community supreme over all individual considerations is a theory for despotism and the snuffing out of humanity. Civil disobedience is a conception that uniquely recognizes both demands of man's nature: the right of the individual to choose what he shall do and the obligation of the individual to abide by whatever legal consequence may be imposed upon him as a result of his choice.

The case against all moral claims for civil disobedience may sound plausible against the background of an open, enlightened, benevolent legal system. Viewed in the light of a possibly different system, the ruling out of all individual rights save those the state sees fit to grant is a frightening prospect. A theory of man or society should serve under other than ideal circumstances in order to command belief. The line between civil disobedience and violent attack on law may be a fine one to draw, and it may remain a serious practical problem to determine on which side of the line a particular act falls. But the line is an important one for us to draw if we intend to make sense of man as a moral and political animal.

NOTES

1. Pp. 50–61 in this volume.
2. Plato, *Apology,* 32 C, D.
3. *Ibid.* 29 C–30 D.
4. Plato, *Crito,* 50 B–51 E.
5. Plato, *Apology,* 30 C.
6. Corporation lawyers become expert in calculating the comparative cost of disobeying laws. The corporation that pays fines in order to reap larger profits is not generally considered criminal in the business world.
7. One device for determining what a law means is deliberately to violate the letter of the law so that the courts have to rule on the applicability of the law. This procedure of bringing a test case, like civil disobedience, is within the bounds of the legal system so long as it is an avowed test and the court decision is accepted or opposed by legal and open means.

II Forms and Uses of Violence

5

The Threat of Violence and Social Change

H. L. NIEBURG

The threat of violence and the occasional outbreak of real violence—which gives the threat credibility—are essential elements in peaceful social change not only in international but also in national communities.[1] Individuals and groups, no less than nations, exploit the threat as an everyday matter. This induces flexibility and stability in democratic institutions.

I refer not only to the police power of the state and the recognized right of self-defense but also to private individual or group violence, whether purposive or futile, deliberate or desperate. Violence and the threat of violence, far from being meaningful only in international politics, are underlying, tacit, recognized, and omnipresent facts of domestic life, in the shadow of which democratic politics are carried on. They instill dynamism into the structure and growth of the law, the settlement of disputes, and

From *The American Political Science Review*, 56 (1962), 865–873. Reprinted (abridged) by permission of the author and publisher.

the processes of accommodating interests, and they induce general respect for the verdict of the polls.

An effort by the state to obtain an absolute monopoly over violence, threatened or used in behalf of private interests, leads inexorably—as in a prison—to complete totalitarian repression of all activities and associations which may, however remotely, create a basis of antistate action. A democratic system preserves the right of organized action by private groups, risking their implicit capability of violence. By intervening at the earliest possible point in private activities, the totalitarian state increases the likelihood that potential violence will have to be demonstrated before it is socially effective. On the other hand, by permitting a pluralistic basis for action, the democratic state permits potential violence to have a social effect with only a token demonstration, thus assuring greater opportunities for peaceful political and social change. A democratic system has greater viability and stability; it is not forced, like the totalitarian, to create an infinite deterrent to all nonstate (and thus potentially antistate) activities. The early Jeffersonians recognized this essential element of social change when they guaranteed the private right to keep and bear arms, in the Second Amendment. The possibility of a violent revolution once each generation is a powerful solvent of political rigidity, making such revolutions unnecessary.

The argument of this essay is that the risk of violence is necessary and useful in preserving national societies. This specifically includes sporadic, uncontrolled, "irrational" violence in all its forms. It is true that domestic violence, no less than international violence, may become a self-generating vortex which destroys all values, inducing anarchy and chaos. Efforts to prevent this by extreme measures, however, only succeed in making totalitarian societies that are more liable to such collapses. Democracies assume the risk of such catastrophes, and thereby make them less likely.

Violence has two inextricable aspects: its actual use (political demonstrations, self-immolation, suicide, crimes of passion, property, or politics, etc.), and its potential (threatened) use. The actual outbreak or demonstration of violence must occur from time to time in order to give plausibility to its threatened outbreak, and thereby to gain efficacy for the threat as an instrument of social and political change. The two aspects, demonstration and threat, therefore cannot be separated. If the capability of actual demonstration is not present, the threat will have little effect in inducing a willingness to bargain politically. In fact, such a threat may instead provoke "preemptive" counterviolence.

The "rational" goal of the threat of violence is an accommodation of interests, not the provocation of actual violence. Similarly, the "rational" goal of actual violence is demonstration of the will and capability of action, establishing a measure of the credibility of future threats, not the exhaustion of that capability in unlimited conflict.[2] An investigation of the function of violence begins with an outline of concepts.

POLITICAL SYSTEMS AND CONSENSUS

We assume that all human relationships, both individual and institutional, are involved in a dynamic process of consensus and competition. These are opposites only as conceptual poles of a continuum. In real relationships, it is often difficult to distinguish objectively between the two. The distinction is sharp only subjectively, for the participant, and his perception of consensus or competition may change from moment to moment, depending on his political role and the objective circumstances.[3] A political role is defined in terms of the many political systems in which the individual objectively or subjectively (by identification of interests) plays a part. A political system contains a hierarchy of authority and values. Each system has a complex structure of leadership and influence but, because of the nature of its task (maximizing and allocating certain values), policy and decision-making power is usually vested in one or a few roles at the top of the pyramid of authority (the elite). Formal and informal political systems exist at all levels of group life (children's play groups, families, lodges, gangs, work groups, nation–state, international alignments, etc.), interpenetrating each other among and between levels. Each isolated system has an interdependent structure of roles, involving loyalty to certain values, symbols, leaders, and patterns of behavior according to system norms. The discrete individual, part of many different systems, must structure his own hierarchy of commitment to meet the simultaneous demands made upon him by many different roles.

Within the individual, the conflicting demands of these roles create tension. Similarly, within each system conflicting values between members are constantly adjusted as roles change, maintaining a state of tension. And political systems as wholes have an objective, dynamic interrelationship, structured into the hierarchy of macrosystems. Within the latter, each subsystem has a role much like that of the individual in smaller constellations. Each subsystem may be part of several macrosystems, imposing conflicting demands upon it. Consequently, within macrosystems there is maintained a state of constant tension between subsystems.

This objective tension, existing on all levels, is perceived subjectively in terms of both competition and consensus, depending on the comparative degrees of collaboration and conflict which exist in the situation at any given moment.

So any two or more systems may appear as hostile at any given time. From the viewpoint of the participants, the conceptual framework of competition overrides underlying consensus. Decisions and policies of the rival elites are then rationalized in terms of hostility to the values and leaders of the other system. However, if events transpire to place a higher value on a hostile tactical situation involving the macrosystem of which both smaller systems are a part, their relationship will be transformed quickly to a conceptual framework of consensus which will override and mute the unresolved competitive elements. Such an event may also bring about internal leadership changes in both subsystems, if their elites were too firmly wedded to the requirements of the now-irrelevant competitive situation.

Objectively, tension is always present among all roles and systems; that is, elements of both competition and consensus go together. The subjective emphasis which each pole of the continuum receives depends on the value which the tactical situation places on acts and attitudes of hostility or collaboration among the various systems at various times. Degrees of hostility and collaboration are structured by a hierarchy of values within and among all roles and systems all the time. All are involved in a dynamic process.

Conflict, in functional terms, is the means of discovering or reaching consensus, of creating agreed terms of collaboration. Because of our personal roles in the macrosystem of nation-states, we tend to view the Cold War in terms of competition. Similarly, because of our roles in the subsystem of the family group, we tend to view family problems in terms of consensus (until the system breaks down completely).

One can reverse these conceptual fields. The Cold War can be viewed in terms of the large areas of consensus that exist between the two power-blocs. For example, the wish to prevent the spread of nuclear weapons to each other's allies; the wish to avoid giving each other's allies the power of precipitating general war between the main antagonists; the common interest in reducing accidental provocations; the common interest in establishing some norms of predictability in each other's behavior; etc. Conflict can therefore be considered merely as the means of perfecting these areas of consensus. In the same way, one can view the family situation negatively in terms of competition and hostility. As in an O'Neill drama, one would dwell on all the things that divide the family members and interpret all actions in terms of maneuvers to subdue each other's will. Consensus then becomes a residual category *hors de combat,* and therefore of no importance. One might dwell upon the collaborative aspects of international affairs or the disruptive aspects of family affairs. A policy-maker should do both in the former area, just as a psychiatrist does both in the latter. The collaborative view of the Cold War should not, however, induce euphoria about the nature of the relationship.

In performing this exercise, the relativistic nature of the concepts of consensus and competition becomes evident. It is impossible to reach any consensus without competition and every consensus, no matter how stable, is still only provisional, since it represents for all its members a submerging of other values. All collaborating individuals, groups, or nations constantly try to exploit favorable opportunities to improve their roles or to impose a larger part of their own value structures upon a larger political system. In an important sense, all individuals, groups, or nations desire to "rule the world," but are constrained to collaborate with others on less desirable terms because of the objective limits of their own power or the cost of the exertion required.

The commitment required to produce a credible threat of violence, sufficient to induce peaceable accommodation, is one of a very high order. Not all individuals or all political systems are capable of credibly using the threat of violence in order to induce greater deference by others to their values. Peoples generally recognize the kinds of values which can and cannot elicit the high degree of commitment required to make the threat credible.

By and large, all violence has a rational aspect, for somebody, if not for the perpetrator. Acts of violence can consequently be rationalized (i.e., put to rational use) whether they are directed against others or against oneself. This is true because people who may be anxious to apply the threat of violence to achieve a social or political bargaining position are nevertheless usually reluctant also to pay the costs or take the risks of an actual demonstration of that threat. Incoherent acts of violence can be exploited by elites as a means of improving their roles or imposing a larger part of their values upon a greater political system. The more obvious the logical connection between such an act and the ends sought by the elite, the easier it is to assimilate the act and claim it as a demonstration of the potential violence available to the elite if its demands are ignored. The rapidity with which insurgent movements create martyrs from the demise of hapless bystanders, and the reluctance of governments to give martyrs to the opposition, are evidence of this.

Nations, Laws, and Ballots

The nation is a highly organized, formal political system whose structure is well defined by law and custom, reinforced by sanctions legally imposed by the near-monopoly violence (police power) of the state. The central problem of lawful societies is to develop principles, procedures, institutions, and expectations that create conditions of continuity and predictability in the lives of their members. The legal system is an abstract model of the society designed to crystallize relationships of the status quo, maintain their continuity in the midst of political and social change, and provide lawful methods of resisting or accommodating change. Law itself tends to maintain the status quo and, with the instruments of state power, to resist change. But relationships in organized societies change anyway. The process for codifying changed conditions and relationships is called "politics." Political systems legitimize certain kinds of potential violence within controlled limits; it then becomes force.[4] However, law almost never serves the interests of all equally. Rather, it protects some against others or gives advantages to some over others. By placing the force of the state behind the interests of some, law serves to neutralize the potential violence behind the demands of others. In a sense, it thus raises the threshold of violence required to make social protests against the law efficacious. This guarantees that the law cannot be changed easily or quickly by any group, thus giving it greater permanence and stability.

Pressures for political and social change must therefore be substantial before the threat of violence and the fear of the breakdown of law and order rise above the threshold set by the force held by the state. While the threat and fear remain below the threshold, the status quo often responds to challenges against the law by more severe enforcement, augmented police, and enlarged prisons. But when the threat and fear come near or cross the threshold, a general tendency toward nonenforcement of the law sets in. The status quo interests begin to share with the disaffected groups a desire to evade and to change the law.

Private demonstrations of force are illegal in all domestic societies. Toleration is accorded to threats of potential violence, however, to the extent that the laws and institutions are democratic. In all systems, the state, to deserve its name, must apply adequate force to control outbreaks of actual violence by private sources—or tolerate some more or less recognized "off-limits" areas for outlawry.[5] If the instrumentalities of state power are not equal to broad private threats, indeed, the government in power ceases to rule. Vigilantism or the private threat of violence has then in fact become the last resort of authority in the system. Why do governments sometimes fall when there is a general strike or a street demonstration? Why don't they ignore outbreaks with which they cannot cope? Why don't they say: "All right, go ahead and strike, fight each other for control of the streets, snake-dance down the avenue. We will sit here in our offices anyway making decisions!" Governments fall when their capabilities for dealing with threatened violence fail. The emerging political system which proves itself capable of raising a higher threshold of violence (than the established government can or will surmount with its force) becomes de facto the highest authority, and de jure the new government.

Laws are not merely the rules of a game of economic and political competition. They are also a means of winning the game, if some of the players can, as in fact they do, write the laws. The ideal system may be one in which the rules are written with perfect dispassion, so that they accord no special advantages to anyone. This ideal is never realized. The process of politics which underlies the making and unmaking of laws is not dispassionate. Indeed, it is one of the most passionate of human affairs. No matter how scrupulously fair may be the original constitution and the representation of governing institutions, the tensions of political systems soon intrude historical hierarchies of advantage. Whoever enjoys early advantages in the game soon enjoys that and more by law, with the heightened threshold of the force available at the beckoning of the state to vouchsafe them. In this manner the law tends always to become to some extent the instrument of the status quo, resisting change.

In democratic societies, however, the law also guarantees the right of voluntary association, among other political liberties, and restrains (by a constitutional distribution of authority) arbitrary use of the police power. These permit opponents of the status quo to establish and maintain a base of political action that may become formidable. It may then be difficult for the regime to find legal pretexts for controlling this base while its potential for antistate violence is still within the state's control capability. Once its potential equals or grows greater than that of the state, repression is no longer a realistic policy. Changing the law, or treating it as a dead letter, gains precedence over enforcing it, even for status quo leaders who wish to preserve what control remains over informal political systems in which they are the elite. Once this process of peaceful political change has been successfully set in motion, both the emerging and the declining political elites have a high interest in maintaining a general freedom to threaten violence without initiating or provoking it, either on the part of the state or by other groups. For the status quo elites, there is more to be gained in preserving the continuity of the laws than in initiating and provoking the demonstration of violence at an unpredictable level. For the insurgent elites, there is usually more to be gained in preserving the continuity of the laws than in appealing to the uncertain results of violence.

In democratic systems, the ballot becomes the nonprovocative symbol by which the elites may measure their capabilities for threatening direct action. In a real sense, voting is an approximation of picking sides before a street fight. Once the sides are picked, the leaders are able to gauge their bargaining strengths and make the best possible deal for themselves and their cohorts. The appeal to actual battle not only is unnecessary, but also, for the weaker side (the only side with an interest in challenging the results of the count), it does not promise to change the results and may in fact undermine the authority of the polls as a method for reversing one's future position.

The threat of violence implicit in counting heads is an ambiguous measure of the power available to the political systems into which people group themselves at election time. The extent of voter commitment in these systems is uncertain and probably, in most cases, unequal to demands for supporting action. There are very few national elections in the United States—although many elsewhere—in which the results prefigure a plausible threat of civil war as the means by which the defeated candidates can gain concessions and appointments from the winning side. In general, democratic political leaders share a common interest in resolving disputes without invoking real violence. Neither side can be confident that the loyalty of its voters will stand the test of a demonstration of strength. Voting is a very imperfect register of loyalty, but rather conveys a miscellany of emotions, difficult to penetrate or to order rationally. Strenuous efforts are made by defeated candidates to restrain a show of violence by their own followers. Public concessions of defeat, homiletic congratulations, and avowals of support for the winner are designed to communicate to their backers the finality of the verdict at the polls, which is subject to revision not by a demonstration of violence but by renewed peaceful efforts in the next election.

THE INTERNATIONAL PROCESS

Many people blithely argue for law as a substitute for violence, as though there were a choice between the two. They call for international law and world government to eliminate war. This point of view reveals a blissful ignorance of the functions of violence in domestic legal systems. A viable system based on law protects the conditions of group action which make threats of violence tolerable. Law always rests on force, a legitimate monopoly in the hands of the state, and it can be changed by the threat of private violence. The threat of violence and the fear of the breakdown of law and order cast their shadows ahead; they operate to moderate demands and positions, thereby setting into peaceful motion the informal political processes of negotiation, concession, compromise, and agreement. Although there is no centralized monopoly of force in the international forum, the processes of mediation and negotiation function in much the same way. The credible threat of violence in the hands of nations has a similarly stabilizing effect, providing statesmen are attentive to the maintenance of their national capability for demonstrating violence and providing their ambitions are commensurate to the bargaining position which their armaments achieve. More comprehensive legal codes and a world government may not improve the stability of the world community in any case, since the possibility of civil conflict exists in all political systems. Civil wars are frequently bloodier and more unforgiving than wars between sovereign nations.

In international politics also the threat of violence tends to create stability and maintain peace. Here the threat is more directly responsive to policy controls. The nation-state has greater continuity than the informal political systems that coalesce and dissolve in the course of domestic social change. The threat of force can be asserted much more deliberately and can be demonstrated under full control, as in "good will" navy visits, army maneuvers near a sensitive border, partial mobilization, etc. Because of the greater continuity of these macrosystems, the national leaders must strive to maintain the prestige of a nation's might and will. If the reputation of a nation's military power is allowed to tarnish, future bargaining power will be weakened. The country may feel obliged to reestablish that prestige by invoking a test of arms as a means of inducing greater respect for its position from other nations. Strong nations prefer to demonstrate their military power peaceably in order that their prestige will afford them the bargaining power they deserve without a test of arms.

Because the threat of international violence is a conscious instrument of national policy, it generally lacks the random character of domestic violence. This means that if the armaments of nations fall out of balance, if the prestige of nations is no longer commensurate with their ambitions, if the will to take the risks of limited military conflicts is lacking, if domestic political considerations distort the national response to external threat, then the time becomes ripe for the outbreak of violence that may escalate out of control.

In general, the dangers of escalating international conflict induce greater, not lesser, restraint on the part of national leaders in their relations with each other. Attempts to achieve infinite security—and consequent irresponsibility—for the nation are as self-defeating as similar attempts for a domestic regime.

The functioning of consensus and competition between nations is not fundamentally different from that of domestic politics. The most striking difference is that in domestic politics the level of centralized force available to the state creates a high threshold of stability against the threats brought to bear within the system by private groups. In the international forum, the closest approximation to such a threshold is the array of decentralized forces available to the great powers. An aggressive power interested in modifying the *status quo* must cross the threshold of its own threat of force in order to induce other powers to choose between concessions to its demands or the cost and risks of an arms race. To the extent that the *status quo* powers are able and willing to pay the costs and take the risks, their own threshold can be raised, depriving the challenger of any political advantages from his investment. When all of the great powers are attentive to the equations of potential violence, no nation can hope to gain conclusive political advantages from an arms race. This situation makes possible international agreements or a tacit consensus for stabilizing arms and bringing about political settlements. Diplomatic ceremonials, like the ceremonials of personal relations which we call "manners," serve to minimize the dangers of provocation and threat in the day-to-day relations between nations.

THE DOMESTIC PROCESS

Underneath the norms of legal and institutional behavior in national societies lies the great beast, the people's capability for outraged, uncontrolled, bitter, and bloody violence. This is common to totalitarian as well as democratic societies and is a major restraint against completely arbitrary government. Even totalitarian regimes can hope for stability only if they reflect in some degree the changing currents of political interest of the people and if they are willing to recruit members of their elites from the potentially disaffected groups which they rule. Even a totalitarian state must purvey some concept of fairness and flexibility, an ability to change in response to the changing internal and external demands put upon it. Indeed, to the extent that a totalitarian regime permits the threat of violence to be raised against it in the form of political pressure, it loses some of its totalitarian quality. The dynamics of totalitarianism, however, generally make this kind of evolution difficult, if not impossible. Dictatorships of one or a few raise the level of official terror to offset or deter the threat of violence from below. Terror and counterterror may escalate until the whole system collapses in an orgy of violence. The prospects for raising anything but another such dictatorship out of such wreckage would seem remote, except that people tire of violence and presently respond to it with passivity. Dictators are sometimes suspected of seeking an escape from this iron logic by provoking international wars which unite the country behind the leader, postponing issues of internal dissension.

The threat to carry political dissent outside peaceable channels can distract the government from the pursuit of other values, can impose upon it as its first and major responsibility the reestablishment of domestic peace and order, and can lure it into shortsighted measures to suppress violence, measures that may instead widen the base of opposition and increase the occasions for antigovernment protests.

The mere threat of private violence directed against the government has a very great influence upon government actions. By causing reallocations of the resources of the society into the essentially negative goals of internal security, the opposition may succeed in defeating or crippling the positive goals whose accomplishment might legitimize and strengthen government authority. To avoid this predicament, even totalitarian governments occasionally go out of their way to appease their critics. The alternative to reform is ruthless suppression not only of the sources of the threat but also of every symptom of united social action.

Bowling clubs, assemblies of three or more people on street corners—there is no rational way to identify the first links of the chain which leads to social action. All must be broken up. The hopeless search for infinite security begins in this way; its logical end is the downfall of the regime. With this choice before it, it is easy to see why even a dictatorial regime may prefer social and political reform to the threat of violence. This is why so many kings and tsars, rather than destroying their rivals and opponents, often sent them instead on enforced vacations and educational tours abroad.

In democratic societies this sharp dilemma is avoided far short of infinite deterrence. The institutional distribution of authority—constitutionalism—precludes unilateral attempts to centralize all the police powers in the hands of one agent. Also, the law proscribes the overt threat of private violence and the existence of paramilitary forces, although it tolerates and protects the implied threat of violent outbreaks if political accommodation fails. Violence is demonstrated, not in organized forms, but rather in sporadic outbursts. Disgruntled elites who possess a clear capability for causing a planned demonstration—who have, that is, organized groups with a deep sense of moral outrage and injustice—avoid incriminating themselves and provoking counteraction against themselves. Instead they carry out "peaceable demonstrations" designed to reveal their numbers and the intensity of their commitment. These may have the bonus effects of provoking violent action against them, causing government intervention, or causing their more inflammable followers to ignite into unplanned outbursts of violence. Such potentials are implicit in the situation.

The leaders of the agitators are then placed in a position of minimum risk and maximum effectiveness, that of playing the role of "responsible leader." They can bargain with formal authorities and with all the other members in this way: "You must accept our just complaints and you must deal with us; otherwise, we will not be able to control our people. Unspeakable things may happen. We do not desire this to happen, but it is up to you to help us prevent it." While playing this role, the reformist lead-

ers may not be unhappy to have their prophecies partially ful-
filled by sporadic outbreaks. Events which demonstrate violence
(and thus induce other elites to make concessions) do not have
to be planned. Once the emotions of a real social movement are
churned up, the problem is to keep the events from happening.

The irresponsible elements may be disowned, but the bargaining power of the responsible leaders is enhanced. In the bargaining process, the moderate leaders often accept concessions which
fall short of those demanded by some of their more extremist
followers. Opportunists or "realists" often inherit the benefits
wrought by the blood of martyrs. This is a healthy mode of exploiting the demonstration of violence without condoning it, enabling compromises to be reached which isolate the extremists
and render them less dangerous to the body politic. Most followers in social movements will follow responsible leadership
through the give-and-take of compromise because they share the
general fear of unlimited violence and counterviolence, with its
unpredictable results and the defeat of all rational goals. Accom-
modations can be reached, even if only provisionally, which preserve the general consensus in maintaining the form and continuity of society and law.

NOTES

1. "Violence" is defined as direct or indirect action applied to restrain,
   injure, or destroy persons or property.
2. By "rational" here is meant: having a conceptual link to a given end,
   a logical or symbolic means–ends relationship which can be demonstrated to others or, if not demonstrable, is accepted by others (but
   not necessarily all) as proven.
3. Essentially, the perception by an individual of his relationship to
   others within a framework of hostility or cooperation is the subjective
   basis of "ideology," using the term as Karl Mannheim does in
   "Sociology of Knowledge," *Ideology and Utopia* (New York: Har-
   court, Brace, 1954), pp. 265–266.
4. The distinction between "violence" and "force" (one uncontrolled,
   the other controlled), was common in pre-Lasswellian literature. They
   are often difficult to distinguish objectively. Assessments of control-
   lability may be almost entirely ideological. I prefer to use "force" to

designate the objective capabilities, i.e., the concrete means or instruments for violence.

5. There are many areas outside the effective—if not the nominal—jurisdiction of formal governmental authority, as, for example, "off-limit" slum areas where police seldom penetrate, or the Mafia areas of Sicily. Such areas represent political subsystems which possess a high degree of sovereignty, tolerated, for one reason or another, by the general government. Within such areas, the de facto authority is often the elite able to maintain the highest threshold of potential violence, not the formal government. In such areas, an unwritten law usually makes it a severely punished offense to call upon the authority of the general government.

6

Violence and the Process of Terror

EUGENE V. WALTER

To investigate terrorism is to study power *in extremis,* and, as sometimes happens when extreme situations are probed for meaning and mechanism, the inquiry raises many questions about power in general, throws a new light on it, and reveals features that are ordinarily invisible in more tranquil conditions. Terror, moreover, is not confined to political systems that are anomalous or exotic. The potential is to be found in ordinary institutions as well as in unusual situations, and reigns of terror are not properly understood if they are conceived exclusively as ephemeral states of crisis produced by adventitious events or as alien forms of control. Systems of terror, usually defined as "abnormal" by the conventions of Western social and

From *American Sociological Review,* 29 (1964), 248–257. Copyright 1964 by the American Sociological Association. Reprinted (abridged) by permission of the author and publisher. (A revised version of this essay appeared in Eugene V. Walter, *Terror and Resistance: A Study of Political Violence* [New York: Oxford University Press, 1969].)

political thought, may be generated under certain conditions of stress by "normal" political processes, and the problem of terror raises virtually every other major issue in political sociology and political theory.

THE CONCEPT OF TERROR

The word "terrorism" conventionally means a type of violent action, such as murder, designed to make people afraid. In ordinary usage, however, the word "terror" is ambiguous, often suggesting any kind of extreme apprehension, without regard to the cause. Moreover, it may mean, on the one hand, the psychic state—extreme fear—and, on the other hand, the thing that terrifies—the violent event that produces the psychic state. I shall try to avoid confusion by maintaining a precise usage, employing terms such as "terrorism" and "organized terror" consistently as equivalents to "process of terror," by which I mean a compound with three elements: the act or threat of violence, the emotional reaction, and the social effects.

This usage makes it clear that the experience of "terror" differs in many ways from other kinds of fear and from anxiety. Whereas anxiety may be caused by a number of factors, including intrapsychic tensions, interpersonal conflicts, and unsettled social conditions, the "terror" examined here is restricted to the emotional state caused by specific violent acts or threats. By "cause," I mean sufficient condition.

To clarify my definition, I shall suggest briefly some limiting cases, showing that the "process of terror" concept excludes several situations that are loosely called "terrorism" or "reign of terror."

For example, imagine a revolution in which the successful insurgents carry out mass executions of former officials and their associates. Suppose, for the sake of illustration, there is no confusion between the revolutionary citizens who, we shall assume, approve the executions, and the adherents to the old regime. In addition, assume that no suspicion of counterrevolutionary activity hangs over the citizens and that the executions do not make them afraid for their own safety. Then the situation can be clearly defined as destructive violence against former power holders, but not as a "process of terror."

For another example, modify the first hypothetical case and imagine that at the same time the executions are taking place, the citizens are faced with widespread famine, disease, great social dislocations, and the threat of invasion. The atmosphere is full of fear existing simultaneously with the mass executions. Yet, the behavior of the revolutionary government is not "terrorism," nor is the relation between leaders and citizens a "system of terror" if the fear is caused by these other factors and not by the executions or similar acts of government violence.[1]

A system of terror may be defined broadly to include certain states of war as well as certain political communities, as long as the term refers to a sphere of relationships controlled by the terror process. To designate such a sphere as a "system of terror," however, implies that all the individuals within it are involved, in one role or another, actually or potentially in the terror process. Hence, a "system of terror" should not be identified as any society that happens to have terror in it. Durable pockets of terrorism, restricted to specific kinds of behavior or to special classes of individuals, may be found enclosed in societies generally governed by more benevolent methods. For example, sedition may be expunged *in terrorem;* felons, slaves, or an ethnic minority may receive exceptional violent treatment, and in such instances we may speak of a zone of terror, within which the violence and fear are confined. Outside the zone, power relations follow the rules of an ordinary system of authority. Whether the sphere is considered as "zone" or as "system" depends on what is understood to be the domain of observation. For example, isolated conceptually and taken as a closed system, slavery of a certain kind is a "system of terror"; however, it is also a "zone of terror" within the society that contains it. This larger society is itself not a "system of terror" unless all the members are involved, in one role or another, actually or potentially in the terror process.

Systems of terror fall into two major categories, depending on whether they work against or coincide with the dominant power structure. One type is oriented toward overthrowing a system of authority—for example, a state—either to enable the directors of the terror staff to seize control of the state or to clear the way for some other group approved by them. In this type, the members of the terror staff may be recruited externally from foreign enemies of the political system under attack, or drawn from indigenous rebels or revolutionaries. Its purpose, in any case, is to destroy the authority system by creating extreme fear through systematic violence. The type may be referred to as a siege of terror and is not the subject of this paper.[2]

Systems of terror in the other category coincide and coact with systems of authority and are directed by those who already control the ordinary institutions of power. Instead of relying entirely on authority, conventional rules, and legitimate techniques, the men in power, for various reasons, choose to initiate the process of terror. The form may be called a regime of terror, and it is understood that the systems of terror discussed in this paper are of this type.

Regardless of its political orientation, the first element of the terror process, in a logical as well as a chronological sense, is the specific act or threat of violence, which induces a general psychic state of extreme fear, which in turn produces typical patterns of reactive behavior. Violence, the principal element of the terror process, should be distinguished from "force," "coercion," and "power," for it is important to understand how terrorism differs from the ordinary political practice of coercion. An analysis of power is beyond the scope of the present essay, but I should indicate that I use the term in its broad sense to include all the forms of influence and compulsion. I shall use the word force to include any agency that compels someone to do something he does not want to do. "Coercion" will be limited to social forms of compulsion—usually some kind of institutionalized force.

The term violence will be restricted to the sense of destructive harm, hence, a destructive kind of force. As a general term it would include not only physical assaults that damage the person, but also magic, sorcery, and the many techniques of inflicting harm by mental or emotional means. One may turn to anthropological literature for accounts of magical and spiritual terrorism practiced by shamans, magicians, and priests.[3] Historically, however, physical violence is more ponderable, more extensive, and tends to be organized on the widest scale. The kind of terrorism examined in this essay depends on the use of physical violence.

THE USES OF VIOLENCE

Some historical periods have the reputation of being filled with violence. Jan Huizinga, in his study of the late middle ages, meditates on the violent tenor of life then, its oscillation between cruelty and tenderness, and the public joy in torture and executions.[4] From the first age of feudal society, after the Frankish Roman Empire broke up, Europe had experienced widespread disorder, but violence was more than a reaction to political disintegration. It was deeply rooted, Marc Bloch tells us, in the social structure and the mentality of the time. Violence was even an element in manners, and medieval men, emotionally insensitive to the spectacle of pain and having small regard for human life, "were very prone to make it a point of honor to display their physical strength in an almost animal way."[5] Violence had become a class privilege for the nobility, which reserved to itself the right of private vengeance and "as a mark of honor any form of recourse to arms."[6]

Violence, then, is not exclusively an instrument of control; it can also be a privilege of social rank. Since I am dealing with violence as an instrument of power, I shall exclude violence that occurs as a mark of status or honor, or for other reasons, such as a disposition to behave in a cruel or intemperate manner. Similarly, I shall exclude economic terrorism, ranging from armed robbery to systematic extortion, and the various methods by which violence may be used for economic gain.

When violence is employed in the service of power, the limit of force is the destruction of the thing that is forced. As Tillich puts it, "In this sense there is an ultimate limit to any application of force. That thing which is forced must preserve its identity. Otherwise it is not forced but destroyed."[7] A violent event, however, may be simply an act of destruction—for vengeance or other reasons, or for no apparent reason. In this case, violence is not an instrument of power, for the violent act is complete and the object destroyed.

We must distinguish, therefore, between the process of violence and an act of destruction which is complete and not an instrument of anything else. The former is incomplete, for it is directed to an end beyond itself—in the cases under discussion, the proximate aim is to instill terror; the ultimate end is control. Thus, in civil terror we are dealing with two processes, one dependent on the other: the process of violence in the service of terror and the process of terror in the service of power.

Military terror is different. When terrorism is used in a war of extermination, the aim is to paralyze the enemy, diminish his resistance, and reduce his ability to fight, with the ultimate purpose of destroying him. In this case, we see the process of violence in the service of terror, and ultimately, terror in the service of violence. The great Zulu despot, Shaka, is an example of one who perfected both civil and military terrorism.

As long as terror is directed toward an end beyond itself, namely, control, it has a limit and remains a process. Under certain conditions, terror becomes unlimited and therefore is no longer a process but an end in itself.

Violence may occur without terror, but not terror without violence. In examining violence designed to control, we should distinguish the process of terror from the use of violence to change conditions. In the former case, the regime does not eliminate the group that falls in the zone of terror, but controls it through violence and fear. A segment of the group may be destroyed to instill terror in the rest, but the group is not wiped out. In the latter case, persons in the zone of violence are destroyed as a group, making a structural change in the society. The latter is an irreversible change, for the selective depletion of the population renders the society that emerges after the violence has ceased structurally different from the society that preceded it. In contrast, the process of terror is reversible, in this special sense, for by itself it does not alter the structural characteristics of the society. The very fact that the fundamental conditions remain unchanged makes the system of terror necessary in the minds of the directors. The following examples will illustrate the difference between the two types.

First, consider a violent process that changes the conditions of control by liquidating a group of persons. Take the hypothetical case of a tyranny opposed by an aristocracy and imagine that instead of meeting aristocratic resistance by concessions or by terror, the regime decides to eliminate the intransigent aristocrats. When the dust settles, they are dead or have fled, the society is now structurally different, and the regime controls without the previous opposition.

In the second case, imagine that the resisters are food producers who cannot be eliminated as a class because they are indispensable. If violence is used against them, it is to keep them in control, and when it ceases, the society remains structurally unchanged.

The two situations are quite different, yet the second type in time may be transformed into the first. Imagine that a process of violence is initiated against a nobility with the intention not of destroying it but of keeping it in control. If the terror continues over a long period of time and a significant number of nobles perish as victims, the nobility is gradually depleted as a class. Their ranks may grow empty, or the places may be filled by the regime with new personnel whose political attitudes are different from those of the liquidated nobles.

A combination of these types is possible. The extinction of Group A, for example, may be used as the process of violence that creates the terror that controls Group B.

Violence and Resistance

Violence, then, may be used to destroy, to control, or to punish. Control and punishment are forms of power, whereas destruction is not, unless it is used indirectly to control or to punish. In conditions of minimal resistance, unless other cultural or psychic factors create a disposition to act in a violent manner, men in authority tend to avoid destructive methods of power. Resistance or the expectation of resistance, on the other hand, increases the probability of violence.

The modes of resistance, as well as the methods of dealing with it, are ways of exercising power. Acts of resistance are acts of counterpower, and the same is true of measures to counter resistance. The forms of resistance are not necessarily violent: they may employ persuasion and other kinds of influence. The same may be said of the techniques employed to counter resistance.

An act of force initiates changes in the behavior of respondents against their will or inclination. The forms of resistance are ways in which the respondents attempt to keep these undesired changes from taking place, or methods of retaliating in some other field of action. I shall mention a few kinds of resistance, using the example of an established power relation between a "superior" and "subordinates."

(1) The subordinates may try to persuade the superior to withdraw the action he initiated. (2) They may simply refuse to obey, risking punishment. (3) They may obey with overt reluctance, creating obstructions that are expensive to the superior. (4) They may try to deter him by threatening punishment. (5) They may punish him by withholding advantages he ordinarily receives (e.g., taxes). (6) They may use violence against the agents who enforce his decision. (7) They may attack the superior himself. (8) By intrigue or some other means they may initiate controls over his conduct in some other field of action. (9) They may initiate actions to change the conditions that moved the superior to take action in the first place.

Resistance to power, then, takes the form of punishment and countercontrol, but a power relation is a dynamic interaction in which at least some control may be exercised by all parties. Of course, each does not control the others to the same degree, nor do they control the same thing. Simmel recognizes that domination is a form of interaction in which the superior generally acts so as to make the subordinate react to him, but in a manner chosen by the superior.[8] Power relations vary in the degree to which the subordinate's act is actually controlled by the superior. The institutional forms through which men control and organize the energies of others permit greater or lesser degrees of autonomy and freedom, and the degree of spontaneity and independence that subordinates bring to the total relaxation conditions whether they are limited in their reciprocal action or whether they are able to resist the superior's will. An established power system is a web of resistances as well as a circuit of controls, and innovators aflame with the *libido dominandi* often take drastic measures to cut through the web.

Even situations of absolute power often contain certain limits imposed by the claims of subordinates. Simmel observes:

> If the absolute despot accompanies his order by the threat of punishment or the promise of reward this implies that he himself wishes to be bound by the decrees he issues. The subordinate is expected to have the right to request something of him; and by establishing the punishment, no matter how horrible, the despot commits himself not to impose a more severe one. . . . The significance of the relation is that, although the superordinate wholly determines the subordinate, the subordinate nevertheless is assured of a claim on which he can insist or which he can waive.[9]

Confrontation, Simmel contends, implies interaction, and in principle interaction always contains some limitation on each party to the process, although there are exceptions to this rule.

History is full of techniques introduced by rulers to manage the conditions of confrontation so as to reduce the potential for reciprocal control by subordinates. One way is to increase the political distance between ruler and subjects: by deifying the ruler or finding other ways to make him unapproachable, or by any method of political mystification drawn from that ancient bag of tricks known as the *arcana imperii*. One of the tasks of the present inquiry is to discover the conditions in which these more subtle methods of dealing with resistance are abandoned for the processes of violence and terror.

Resistance may be countered by persuasion; by rewards and "buying off" leaders of the opposition; by negotiation, bargain-

ing, and exchanging advantages; and by forms of coercion short
of violence. Acts that are not violent but which control through
fear may be distinguished from the process of terror and defined
as "intimidation." This technique includes economic and social
deprivation, and may be described as follows:

> Intimidation as a means of achieving desired ends is a feature
> of behavior where power or authority is based primarily and
> essentially on force. . . . It calls for a technique calculated to
> evoke fear in the party which is expected to do or not to do
> certain things, without, however, resorting to direct violence,
> which would bring intimidation into conflict with established
> authority and law.[10]

In certain institutions that set the acceptability of resistance
near zero, the method of control, frequently resorting to violence, stands at the edge of the terror process. Slavery is such an
institution. Theodor Mommsen in his great history of Rome re-
marks that "slavery is not possible without a reign of terror."[11]
Stanley Elkins persuasively compares some of the techniques of
North American slavery to those of the Nazi concentration
camp.[12] In the antebellum American South, Kenneth Stampp
shows, slavemasters developed an elaborate power system that
depended on complex techniques to minimize resistance.[13] Although most masters seemed to prefer persuasion and reward to
punishment, violence was regarded as a necessary means of control and punishment.

> Without the power to punish, which the state conferred upon
> the master, bondage could not have existed. By comparison, all
> other techniques of control were of secondary importance. . . .
> But the whip was the most common instrument of punishment—
> indeed it was the emblem of the master's authority.[14]

The violence of punishment, however, easily shifted over to the
violence of terrorism, for the process was used not only to punish acts of disobedience and resistance but also to sap the potential for disobedience in advance and break the power to resist.
Brutality was common on large plantations, and the typical over-

seer preferred physical force to incentives as a method of governing slaves. "Some overseers, upon assuming control, thought it wise to whip every hand on the plantation to let them know who was in command." Slaves had to be flogged, it was sometimes maintained, until they manifested "submission and penitence." The lash was often used to "break in" young slaves and to "break the spirit" of insubordinate older ones.[15]

Violent treatment is encouraged by ways of thinking that dehumanize classes of persons or reduce them to objects. Resistance is not acceptable from an instrument. A tool that refuses to carry out the purposes of its owner is defective, and it is either discarded or hammered into shape.

The technical concept of the slave classifies him as a tool—an idea clearly expressed in the theory of slavery found in ancient treatises on agriculture. The often quoted Varro, for example, classifies implements of cultivation in three categories: (1) *genus vocale,* those having speech; (2) *genus semi-vocale,* those having voices that are not articulate; (3) *genus mutum,* the silent ones. The first category includes the slaves; the second, the oxen; and the third, the wagons.[16] If the technical conception of the slave as an instrument of production prevails over other moral or humane notions, then economic factors determine his conservation or destruction.

Hannah Arendt points out the consequences when the notions drawn from areas of productivity invade the understanding of control and authority:

> an element of violence is inevitably inherent in all activities of making, fabricating, and producing, that is, in all activities by which men confront nature directly, as distinguished from those activities, like action and speech, which are primarily directed toward human beings. The building of the human artifice always involves some violence done to nature—we must kill a tree in order to have lumber, and we must violate this material in order to build a table.[17]

Therefore, when control is confused with notions of fabricating and building, people may be viewed not only as instruments but also as materials to be shaped according to design. Resistance from this viewpoint may be interpreted as the unyielding property of a stubborn material.

From the point of view of one who uses violence to cope with it, resistance may be perceived as the premeditated activity of determined political opposition, or, on the other hand, it may appear as the irrational behavior of people too stupid, too backward, too barbarous, or too fractious to respond to methods of control more subtle than violence. For analytical purposes, resistance should be understood objectively as an organized response to a force that provokes it, and also subjectively, according to the meanings given to it by both parties to the conflict.

VIOLENCE AND WAR

In the present age, governments have to deal with *satyagraha* campaigns and organized civil disobedience. These movements have been styled by the sociologist Clarence Marsh Case as forms of "nonviolent coercion." They seek to bring changes against the will of the power holders, but with acts that are not destructive.[18] Although the participants may renounce coercion as well as violence, and though they may intend their efforts as a pure attempt at persuasion, such campaigns are nevertheless interpreted as organized acts of force opposing official actions. The resisters, of course, interpret the official actions they are opposing as initial acts of force.

Because a resisting group is generally weaker than the group that exercises power, and because in a modern power system the former group does not usually have effective instruments of violence, reactions to resistance are more frequently violent than acts of resistance. Discussing African resistance movements, Leo Kuper observes:

> Passive resistance and Mau Mau are very different forms of resistance adopted, in recent years, by the indigenous peoples of Africa against the domination of white settler groups. The response of the dominant group in Kenya to the primitive violence of Mau Mau is the counterviolence of modern warfare, while

in South Africa the white rulers have responded to passive resistance, not directly by violence, but by the establishment of the necessary machinery for violent action.[19]

When organized resistance uses destructive techniques employing instruments of violence, and it is met with similar violent actions, then the confrontation may be defined as warfare.

War, according to the classic formulation by Clausewitz, is a duel on an extensive scale between armed combatants, each striving by physical violence to compel the other to submit to his will, and each aiming to overthrow the adversary and make him incapable of further resistance.

> War, therefore, is an act of violence to compel the enemy to fulfill our will.
> Violence, to encounter violence, equips itself with the inventions of art and science. . . . Violence, i.e., physical violence . . . is therefore the means; imposing our will on the enemy, the end.[20]

War is a political instrument, Clausewitz continues, carrying out political transactions by violent means, and it is an act of violence practiced without limits.[21] The aim of all action in war is to disarm the enemy and remove his ability to resist, and victory in battle consists in nothing less than the physical and moral destruction of the enemy's armed forces.[22] War resembles the process of terror in many ways, but Clausewitz provides the clue for distinguishing the two. "War," he writes, "is not the action of a living force on a lifeless mass, but . . . always the shock of two living forces colliding."[23]

VIOLENCE AND PUNISHMENT

Military terrorism, as a technique of warfare, is within Clausewitz's conception, but civil terror, as previously defined, is frequently practiced against unarmed, noncombatant populations by their own leaders. If the directors of the terror are interested in self-justification, the practice may take place under the guise of legal punishment and the enforcement of law.

This raises the question of when violence inflicted by men in authority is legal punishment and when it is not. As I have indicated, in the institution of slavery, punishment easily changes to terrorism. Since violent punishments do evoke fear and are often justified by their putative deterrent value, it is sometimes hard to distinguish the administration of punishment from the process of terror. It is more difficult when political leaders use the violence involved in the act of punishment to extend their political control. In such cases, the violence *seems* to serve the separate processes of punishment and terror simultaneously.

When a violent process is socially prescribed and defined as a legitimate means of control or punishment, according to the practices familiar to us, the destructive harm is measured and the limits made clear. Social definition as an authorized method often extracts it from the category of violence—at least from the standpoint of the society—and places it in the same domain with other socially approved coercive techniques.

Thus, violence is generally understood as unmeasured or exaggerated harm to individuals, either not socially prescribed at all or else beyond established limits. It is often socially defined to include processes that originate as authorized, measured force but go beyond the prescribed conditions and limits. For example, in systems such as ours, a police officer may be authorized to exercise physical restraint in making an arrest, but he will be said to act in a violent manner if, without acceptable reasons, he attacks and injures a fugitive. In some cases however, police brutality may be officially condemned as violence, yet socially expected and used unofficially as a means of control. In this study, any kind of destructive harm will be taken as violence, but specified as legitimate or illegitimate by social definition. Terrorism is distinguished by the conditions, the structure, and the effects of the violent process.

In the oldest forms of punishment, it has been suggested in some historical studies, the violent destruction of the offender serves the purpose of removing a source of danger from the community. In the earliest stages of primitive society, punishment is entirely defensive, and the violence not intended to produce suffering or fear.[24] Deterrence, the argument continues, was introduced in the later stage by kings and despots, who tended to deal with crimes as offenses to the royal office:

> The ruler is not slow to discover that one of the most effective means of safe-guarding his interests is to strike terror into his subjects, and the principle of determent manifests itself in those horrible mutilations and refined cruelties characteristic of the penal system of absolutism.[25]

It is possible, however, to sort out civil punishment from civil terror; Hobbes, who wrought with great care the deterrence rationale of punishment, also provides the key to the distinction.

In *Leviathan,* describing the characteristics of punishment, Hobbes distinguishes it from an act of hostility. Punishment applies only to persons already in a condition of political obedience to the authority that inflicts it. Against enemies, including those who by rebellion renounce their status as subjects, any degree of violence is permitted:

> Harme inflicted upon one that is a declared enemy, fals not under the name of Punishment: Because seeing they were either never subject to the Law, and therefore cannot transgresse it; or having been subject to it, and professing to be no longer so, by consequence deny they can transgresse it, all the Harmes that can be done them, must be taken as acts of Hostility. But in declared Hostility, all infliction of evil is lawfull.[26]

Punishment, in contrast to an act of hostility, has certain limitations and defining characteristics, and its purpose is to strengthen the disposition to obey:

> A Punishment is an Evill inflicted by publique Authority, on him that hath done, or omitted that which is Judged by the same Authority to be a Transgression of the Law; to the end that the will of men may thereby the better be disposed to obedience.[27]

Hobbes proceeds to list a number of conditions that extract inflicted evils from the class of punishments and give them the character of hostile acts. Among these conditions, penalities that are inflicted without previous public judicial process, or for an act that took place before there was a law to forbid it, or in excess of the penalties prescribed and published in the law, lose the character of punishments. Likewise, all evil inflicted without the intention or the possibility of disposing the offender, or by his example, other men, to obey the laws is not punishment but an act of hostility, "because without such an end, no hurt done is contained under that name."[28]

Punishment defined sociologically, I would maintain, means a penalty imposed for the transgression of a recognized norm established either by coercion or consent in the course of a social relationship. The features that distinguish violent legal punishment from other kinds of violence, including the terror process, are fundamental conditions of legality. For violence to qualify as legal punishment, it must be imposed by duly constituted public authority for an act within its jurisdiction that is publicly judged to violate a legal rule promulgated before the act took place. In addition, the penalty must not exceed that stated in the law, and according to Hobbes, at least, as well as the utilitarians who follow him, it must be inflicted with the intention or the reasonable probability that it will strengthen the disposition to obey the laws. These conditions of legality are limits to violence, and if they are indeed observed, no matter how harsh the punishment —although, certainly, severe punishment may be condemned on other grounds—it is excluded from the category of terrorism. Violence, in these conditions, would follow deviation from the rule, and no matter how destructive punishment might be, the individual who chooses to conform remains reasonably secure from official harm. In contrast, the terror process begins with violence, which is followed by intense fear and irrational, reactive behavior patterns.

In contrast to terrorism, deterrence implies the anticipation of a probable evil and the ability to avoid it. The fear of punishment is different from the fear generated in the terror process. There is a great deal of difference between the emotional state of a man who can calculate, "I fear that if I take this course of action, it will lead to violent punishment," and the turbulent, irrational fear, scarcely permitting thought, stirred up in the wake of the process of violence.

The conditions of legality imply that there must be a way of being innocent. If no path is left open to avoid transgression, or if people are bound to be charged falsely with offenses they did not commit, then it is not possible to be innocent. In the terror process, no one can be secure, for the category of transgression is, in reality, abolished. Anyone may be a victim, no matter what action he chooses. Innocence is irrelevant.

CONCLUSION

Terrorism differs from war and punishment in the way violence is used. The violent process may be a means of destruction, an instrument of punishment, or a method of control, and it may shift from war to terrorism, to punishment, and back. The mere presence of violence is not as significant as the degree of violence, the occasions for its official use, and its place in the temporal sequence of the process used in the service of power.

One could construct a typology of power systems based on the use of violence. At one pole are systems that use violence as a last resort, at the other, those that use it as a first measure. Somewhere between them belong the Draconian systems, which punish the smallest infractions with the severest violence, yet do not extend the use of violence beyond punishment. Were we to fill out this skeleton with the flesh of historical experience, we could identify at one pole the systems blessed with concord, in which power is supported by minimal force, and in which violence is truly an *ultima ratio*. At the other extreme, we should find the terror systems in which violence is a *prima ratio potestatis.*

Every state has the necessary conditions for terrorism, namely, a staff of men obedient to the directors of the system and equipped with instruments of violence, as well as a population capable of experiencing fear. The sufficient conditions invite our exploration, and we must search for them. To identify controlling factors, we may construct a ladder going from actual to potential terrorism, with three levels: (1) situations in which terrorism is being practiced; (2) situations in which the agents of violence are not practicing terrorism at the time, but nevertheless are disposed to initiate violence if people were to behave in a certain way; (3) situations in which terror is absent, but in which there is a threshold of stress beyond which an armed staff will be converted into a terroristic apparatus and a regime of terror established.

The practice in authoritarian states of punishing definite acts of resistance and breaking up organizations suspected of sedition may be compared to a surgical procedure. In contrast, the process of terror, in its ideal form, may be compared to a chemical procedure. Independent social clusters and unauthorized political associations tend to dissolve in the medium of extreme fear. More than that, however, an emotional environment is created in which certain kinds of interaction cannot take place. The first efforts from which organized opposition might emerge are simply not made. The steps that might lead to confrontation with the agents of violence are never taken. Unless they are insulated in some unusual manner from the corrosive process, the people in such an environment are deprived of a capacity that naturally belongs to the members of other systems—the power of resistance.

No historical system, judging from the results, has managed to eliminate resistance completely. In the concentration camps, the Nazis came closest to perfecting the system of terror in many respects; still, the camps fell short of their intentions. No system of terror, despite its enormous horror and devastation, has proved to be entirely effective. Likewise, it should go without saying that no empirical system is wholly congruent with the ideal type. But before any investigation turns to the historical variations, with their unique characteristics and particular differences, it is important to grasp the ideal type.

Furthermore, in a general study of the kind I have projected, it is important to keep free of the mental set that tends to restrict the terror process to systems of total power. To be sure, some of the best theoretical work on terror available today is a by-product of studies of totalitarian regimes. Nevertheless, if future research is to reveal protean terror in its full complexity, it requires a broad, unrestricted, comparative approach, which suggests getting some distance from immediate historical experience and viewing the process at work not only in other times but also in several cultures. Distance, objectivity, and new perspectives should contribute to a better understanding of the terror process, which has become so significant in the present age. The human hope of coming to terms with fear by analysis and reflection and the scientific task of formulating a general theory of terror both urge the inquirer over a broad field of experience, where it may be possible to uncover the hidden mechanisms of terror, and, for practical as well as theoretical reasons, learn not only its causes and functions but also the secrets of its termination.

NOTES

1. The "causal" relation in some cases is not obvious. It is far from simple in such instances to evaluate the contributing factors. Despite the difficulty, extracting "causes" from events is a matter for historical and social judgment. One need not conclude from the dense complexity of social processes that all reasoning about sufficient conditions ought to be abandoned.
2. Forms of terrorism in this general category are examined in Brian Crozier, *The Rebels* (London: Chatto and Windus, 1960). See also the League of Nations documents recording the work of several committees, international conferences, and conventions for the repression of terrorism. The list may be found in Hans Aufricht, *Guide to the League of Nations Publications* (New York: Columbia University Press, 1951), pp. 280–281.
3. See Paul Radin, *The World of Primitive Man* (New York: Grove Press, 1960), chaps. 6, 8.
4. Jan Huizinga, *The Waning of the Middle Ages,* trans. F. Hopman New York: Doubleday Anchor, 1954), chap. 1.
5. Marc Bloch, *Feudal Society,* trans. L. A. Manyon (Chicago: University of Chicago Press, 1961), p. 411.
6. *Ibid.,* p. 127.
7. Paul Tillich, *Love, Power, and Justice* (New York: Galaxy Books, 1961), p. 46.
8. *The Sociology of Georg Simmel,* trans. Kurt H. Wolff (Glencoe, Ill.: Free Press, 1950), pp. 181 ff.

9. *Ibid.*, pp. 186–187.
10. J. B. S. Hardman, "Intimidation," *Encyclopedia of the Social Sciences,* vol. 8, p. 239. Cf. Hardman's article "Terrorism," *ibid.,* vol. 14, p. 575, in which he describes terrorism as "the method whereby an organized group or party seeks to achieve its avowed aims chiefly through the systematic use of violence."
11. Theodor Mommsen, *The History of Rome,* 4th ed., trans. W. P. Dickson (New York: Scribner's, 1891), vol. 3, p. 105.
12. Stanley M. Elkins, *Slavery* (Chicago: University of Chicago Press, 1959), chap. 3.
13. Kenneth M. Stampp, *The Peculiar Institution* (New York: Knopf, 1956), chap. 5.
14. *Ibid.*, pp. 171, 174.
15. *Ibid.*, pp. 183, 177.
16. Marcus Terentius Varro, *Rerum Rusticarum,* I. xvii.1. See also Edmund H. Oliver, *Roman Economic Conditions to the Close of the Republic* (Toronto: University of Toronto Press, 1907).
17. Hannah Arendt, "What Was Authority?" in C. J. Friedrich, ed., *Authority* (Cambridge, Mass.: Harvard University Press, 1958), p. 91.
18. Clarence Marsh Case, *Non-Violent Coercion* (New York: Century, 1923); see also Joan Bondurant, *Conquest of Violence* (Princeton, N. J.: Princeton University Press, 1958), p. 9.
19. Leo Kuper, *Passive Resistance in South Africa* (New Haven: Yale University Press, 1960), p. 72.
20. General Karl von Clausewitz, *Vom Kriege* (13. Aufl.), (Berlin and Leipzig: Vehr's Verlag, 1918), pp. 3–4. The translation is my own; emphases in the original are removed.
21. *Ibid.*, pp. 5, 19.
22. *Ibid.*, p. xxxi.
23. *Ibid.*, p. 6.
24. Heinrich Oppenheimer, *The Rationale of Punishment* (London: University of London Press, 1913), p. 172.
25. *Ibid.*, pp. 174–175.
26. Thomas Hobbes, *Leviathan* (London: Oxford University Press, 1947), p. 241.
27. *Ibid.*, p. 238.
28. *Ibid.*, p. 240.

III

Symbolic
Violence or
Creative Conflict?

7 *Evolution and Revolution*

ERNEST JONES

I suppose that the criteria which would most readily
come to mind in distinguishing a revolutionary from an evolutionary social change are the *speed* with which it was brought
about, the *scale and importance* of the change, and the *violence*
of the means used to effect it. Now let us see how these criteria
really apply to the facts. In the first place we have to distinguish
between political, social, and material revolutions. Such a distinction has this much artificial in it that it is hard to get one
without the others following in its train. Perhaps the political
revolution is the one that comes nearest to existing in a relatively
pure form. When it does, however, we often do not call it a revolution; it somehow does not seem important enough.

Some revolutions at least are only modifications of evolution
and we may put the instructive question: Is this true of all revolutions and, if not, what is the difference between those of which
it is true and those of which it is not?

From *The International Journal of Psychoanalysis,* 22 (1941), 193–208. Reprinted (abridged) by permission of the author's estate and the publisher.

111

Let us turn now to revolutions of a different order, namely, material revolutions. I will mention two of them. The great Industrial Revolution in England was most active from the middle of the eighteenth to the middle of the nineteenth century, although its operations extended a century before and a century after this period. Though essentially of a technical nature, it brought with it vast social and considerable political changes. One has only to think of the displacement of the landed gentry by the new plutocracy, the extension of the suffrage, and so on. In our own days we have seen a somewhat similar revolution initiated by Benz's discovery of the internal combustion engine. This has led to an ever increasing tempo in daily life, to a greater informality in dress and social manners, to an extensive urbanizing of the country, and, above all, to the loosening or destruction of local topographical bonds through the greater ease of communications. Now it will be noted that these material revolutions do not satisfy very well the criteria from which we started. They were not accomplished swiftly nor were they brought about by means of violence. They were not, it is true, entirely dissociated from violence. In the former revolution many lives were lost in industrial rioting against the new machinery, while the complacency with which we regard the horrific annual slaughter on our roads betokens an attitude toward violence which psychologically is not altogether remote from a willingness to inflict it. Furthermore, at least in the industrial revolution, a ruthlessness was manifested which in its callous disregard for human suffering, and in its replacement of beauty by ugliness, could only have proceeded from a group of instinctual activities similar to that which in other circumstances results in open violence. Perhaps it is the dim perception of this feature that makes us unhesitatingly apply the term revolution to a process which at first sight would appear to differ greatly from the other changes we class as revolutionary.

The French Revolution of 1789 and the Russian Revolution of 1917 are perhaps the best examples of social revolutions. Naturally they brought with them both political and material changes as well, but essentially they aimed at changing the social relationships subsisting between different classes in the community, the French one by attacking the social privileges of certain classes, the Russian one by attacking what is called the exploiting powers of certain classes. Of the three classes of revolution the social one undoubtedly evokes the most bitterness and hatred, a fact which leads us directly to consideration of the essential nature of revolution.

I would here put forward the thesis that revolutionary changes are, with a single exception, evoked by the identical forces that bring about evolutionary ones. We have seen that the element of time is not decisive: revolutionary changes may take centuries to produce their effect, while evolutionary ones need not necessarily demand a notably long period for their action. The vastness of the scale may be similar in both, even if this feature is sometimes more visibly striking with the revolutionary changes. The element of violence is not always prominent in revolutionary changes nor always absent from evolutionary ones. At most the degree of tension preceding the change may vary somewhat in the two cases.

Yet the exception I hinted at is of profound significance. What really marks off revolutionary changes in the strict sense from evolutionary ones is the feature of *destructiveness*. The practical test of its presence is whether the former and now displaced conditions are permitted to survive and coexist with the new ones, or at least are transformed in such a fashion that their essential elements persist even if in a new guise (I owe this formulation to my son, Mervyn Jones). When the avowed object of the change is the annihilation of something that went before, and the consignment of it to complete oblivion, then we can truly speak of a revolution.

Bernard Shaw was doubtless right in saying that anyone under the age of thirty who is sensitive to life must be a revolutionary; it is the natural path to manhood. But what does that mean in the language of the unconscious? Surely no more and no less than the impulse of youth to displace the old, or, more specifically, the oedipus wish to kill the father. It is often charged against revolutionaries that they crave for change for the sake of change rather than from a true desire for the new, and this charge is commonly enough borne out in the pathetic, and indeed tragic, feature of revolutions that the leaders after their success tend to reproduce just the attributes of their predecessors against which they had most vehemently inveighed: again we may quote a simple example of this from Russia, where the Cheka, later the Ogpu, exactly reproduced the notorious "Third Section" or Ochrana of the later Czarist regime, the descendant of the Oprichnina of Ivan the Terrible. We know that the attitude of the boy to his father is usually an ambivalent one, composed on the one hand of admiration with the desire to emulate him and on the other hand of hostility with the desire to replace him. The influence of the paternal figure may be so great that the boy, instead of developing something new and individual wherewith to express his own personality, often aims at simply displacing the father with the object of reigning in his stead in the same fashion as his father did and with his same attributes.

We know that a revolution is no time for timid leaders, and we are familiar with the tendency of power to pass into the hands of extremists, those who have no compunction in taking matters to the uttermost point—that of murder of the father figure. We are also familiar with the tendency to subsequent reactions and successful counterrevolutions which—as with the Restoration of 1660—are often joyfully greeted by the populace. Both these features are intelligible in the light of the oedipus complex. Those in a state of misgiving attempt half measures which are swept away by the more full-blooded rebels. Then comes the later wave of remorse that favors the counterrevolution unless the previous regime, as in Russia, had become completely despicable.

The most interesting question, however, and by far the most important one sociologically, is why it is that some revolutionaries are content with seizing power and changing social or political conditions while others are possessed with a fury of destructiveness that cannot contemplate any continued existence of the things displaced. Whence this bitter hatred and intolerance, the effects of which are always regretted by later generations who realize what they have lost forever? We find the same contrast in our patients. With some the oedipus complex follows a straightforward path of development which enables the individual to oppose, resist, fight, and even dispossess his various rivals in life with a relatively easy conscience: it is of the essence of life that every generation strives to measure itself with, and where possible surpass, the preceding one. With others the matter is more grim. For them life is not a game, or even a battle, but a very deadly affair in which everything is at stake—something that is more than life itself. They take very literally the old saying: all is fair in love and war. And they are prone to descend to the most malicious and underhand ways of gratifying their hate, gloating over the discomfiture or destruction of their opponent and trampling with fury on his remains or possessions. To what can we ascribe this remarkable difference in the two cases?

The maliciousness, hatred, and often cowardice that so characterize the destructive type of revolutionary indicate, as indeed we find in our actual clinical practice, that such a person has not less sense of guiltiness, but more, than the more moderate variety. Something, therefore, must have happened internally to allow him to pursue his murderous aim with the callousness, ruthlessness, and apparent freedom from guiltiness that are the attributes of the typical destructive revolutionary. The sense of guilt in such people has been disposed of, or successfully kept at bay, by their developing in a specially high degree the paranoid mechanism of projection. They have persuaded themselves that their opponents are so unspeakably evil that they deserve no better fate than torture and death and that to inflict this, so far from being a guilty act, is a laudable one. In their state of exalted conviction they find it easy, in certain circumstances, to infuse a following with both dread of the wicked enemy and loathing for him, and at the same time to inspire them with confidence that if they follow their noble leader the good cause must triumph. We reach thus the conclusion that a successful revolutionary must be more than a little mad.

I will now pass to the problem of social evolution. This is in the first place bound up with the question of social progress. In the second half of the last century few would have doubted the reality and solidity of not only social progress but also human progress. The difference between the assumedly bestial cave man on the one hand, with his savage propensities and his almost certainly undainty behavior at the dinner table, and the refined Victorian gentleman on the other hand was so very striking that it was hard not to regard them as essentially different beings and to preen oneself on the enormous change that had come about in our species in the past 10,000 years. Today our perspective is in many ways different. We know now that in all probability there were high civilizations 10,000 or perhaps more years ago, and that the species *homo* may well be a million years old. More critically objective standards have been applied to the nature of different culture levels. And, last but not least, we have seen in our own generation famous civilizations deteriorate to a level that would have been completely unbelievable forty or fifty years ago, to a level that has only occasionally been reached in the history of mankind. All this must make us very skeptical about identifying social with human progress, for it is certain that great social changes can be brought about without in any way altering man's essential nature.

When speaking of revolutionary changes I called attention to the destructive elements that so often accompany them and said nothing about the creative, altruistic, and idealistic elements that are at least as important. It is generally found more convenient to treat these in connection with the process of evolution, but I want to guard against simply identifying the destructive elements with revolutionary changes and creative ones with evolutionary ones. Both may be operative in either kind of change, which is why I do not make the usual sharp distinction between the two kinds. I consider the positive motives fundamentally similar with both, although I do think that the circumstances accompanying revolution tend specially to favor the action of destructive forces and that when that is so, the amount of destruction is usually grosser and more irreparable than it is in evolutionary changes. At all events let us now inquire into the nature of the idealistic and creative forces, those which are often called the forces of progress.

The outstanding discovery of psychoanalysis in this context has been that many—and some analysts would be inclined to say all—of the original discoveries and betterments and improvements of all kinds that previously were attributed to the action of purely creative impulses are rather to be regarded as by-products resulting from the action of certain defensive mental mechanisms. The endeavor to escape from unconscious guilt and anxiety leads to infinitely varied mental activities, some of which produce what may socially be called "improvements." To the idealism and self-esteem of mankind it is a chastening reflection that so much of what he is most proud of is merely an accidental result of the flight from fear and pain, that a bad conscience should prove to be one of the prime motors in even our loftiest strivings. Still, if it is true we must make the best of it and learn modesty in the process. I would warn, however, against premature generalizing in this matter. While it appears to be true that the genesis of idealistic and altruistic strivings is much more complex than used to be thought, and that in this genesis what may be called negative, reactive, or defensive agents undoubtedly play an important part, that does not at all exclude the operation of more purely positive, creative agents—broadly speaking, those emanating from the love instinct—which indeed may well be factors in guiding the former set into less egotistic directions. The discovery of the importance of hate, for example, does not necessarily diminish the importance of love: it may even enhance it.

The evidence at present available goes to show that both evolutionary and revolutionary movements affecting a community are extensions of mental processes that are essentially individual in origin. By this I mean that individuals, in attempting to deal with their personal (and therefore family) conflicts, make use of the idea of society in general as a region where their conflicting impulses may be depicted, expressed, or worked out.

The saint, as distinct from the ascetic, does not cope with the evil of the world; he averts his gaze with a sigh. Nietzsche said once: "Where one can no longer love, one should pass by." At the other extreme we have the personality whose internal turmoil is so vehement that it can be dealt with only by provoking and thus reproducing a corresponding violent turmoil in the outer world. Such a person makes the typical social agitator or, on another level, the nihilistic *revolutionary*. Between these extremes there is the dissatisfied meliorist, whose restitutive impulses acting in a piecemeal fashion make him into a *social reformer*.

The reason why these distressed personalities become people with a pronounced attitude toward the universe, or, more strictly, toward society, is that the fundamental mechanisms of introjection and projection permit extensive displacements. In the place of the parents who are alternately loved and injured, or toward whom complex processes of restitution are set in motion, there appears the concept of society as a whole with all its rich "good" and "bad" components. The impulses of love and hate, or reparation and restitution, together with the sense of guilt and the ever-present anxiety, undergo a tremendous socialization. The person is convinced that what he is thinking or feeling began with the idea of society and solely refers to it. He is quite unaware that only a part of it really relates to society and that the greater part was generated in a more personal field, that of his attitude toward himself (his body and its impulses) and his parents, a field which has now been replaced by the social one.

The further question is in what circumstances do these socialized motives of individuals coalesce to produce mass effects? I will only say in regard to this that the hope and sense of omnipotence which leaders offer naturally make their greatest appeal when the opposite attitudes are widely prevalent, namely depression (with perhaps despair) and the sense of inferiority or unlovedness. We know from the psychology of individuals that the presence of these attitudes indicates a deep-seated sense of guilt which is being inadequately met by other measures. The source of this guilt is sometimes a sociological problem, but we have to remember the latent sense of guilt in all human beings which is apt to be stirred by any great misfortune or privation. The Hebrew custom of meeting misfortune by having recourse to sackcloth and ashes was a frank recognition of this, but more often the sense of guilt is denied and replaced by projective accusations against others in an attempt to ward off unhappiness and feelings of inferiority. In short, the preliminary condition necessary to the emergence of a forceful leader is suffering. Whereas, however, the saint responds with a "Come unto me, all ye that labor and are heavy laden, and I will give you rest," the leader of revolt cries "Follow me, and I will give you revenge on those who caused your misfortunes." In the latter case evolution becomes revolution.

It is evident that most of what we prize as civilization and culture, whether in the sphere of knowledge or in that of social institutions such as law and religion, has been laboriously acquired by individuals, made the common property of their fellows, and then passed on to successive generations each of which has to acquire it afresh. It is only the ignorant who suppose that a garage mechanic, because he can use the telephone and manipulate an internal combustion engine, is intrinsically superior to, or has a better brain than, an Athenian gentleman of the fifth century B.C. who had none of the requisite knowledge at his disposal. And in the course of millennia knowledge and social institutions grow to a high level and are again and again utterly destroyed. The sole agency that can preserve them from such a fate is a continuous tradition; if this is badly interrupted most or all is lost and mankind has once more to resume its painful efforts. Calamities of nature, such as those leading to famine, may thus interrupt the continuity, but much more potent are the human activities of war and revolution. Most, and possibly all, that distinguishes us from primitive man, what we treasure most highly and preciously, is safeguarded by one thing only—*continuity of tradition*. This is a consideration often lost sight of, but always at a heavy cost.

8

Creative Conflict and the Limits of Symbolic Violence

JOAN V. BONDURANT

Perhaps in no other period of history has rapid social and political change commanded the attention of so many over so broad a spectrum and with such intensity. Involvement and participation have come to be held as both politically expedient and morally desirable. Action is now the central consideration. But action toward what end? And action through what means? These are surely the interrelated key questions. The means adopted for bringing about change must be carefully examined in relation to the objectives of desired change lest the acts arising from participation and involvement be perverted into simple destruction of basic values as well as of established institutions.

There is some irony in the persistent attacks by self-styled revolutionists upon precisely that form of government which provides the flexibility necessary for continuing change. Extremists on both the left and right would pull down representative de-

mocracy which, in itself, constitutes both an end and a means.[1]
Others, who grow impatient with the processes inherent in traditional democratic institutions, are also often moved to act in
such a way that they advance upon revolutionary objectives
without a solid program to offer, with little knowledge of viable
alternative forms of government, and with even less concern to
devise new and effective machinery to replace that which their
actions threaten to destroy. As they engage in demonstrations—
whether designed only to confront the police, to appeal to the
hitherto uninvolved, or forthrightly to undermine institutions—
all claim for their acts an idealism and moral rectitude with
which, they seem to say, there can be no compromise. These en-
gagements in direct action and the claims made by those who
pursue them raise many questions. Among them are those relating to violence, especially as violence has tended to replace earlier efforts at nonviolent action. Even more elusive is the rarely
stated problem arising from symbolic violence and its frequent
use in activist movements directed toward rapid or immediate
change.

It is not difficult to understand the man who takes up the
weapons of violence to destroy whatever appears to him to be
immoral and unjust. For violence is a time-honored mode of
fighting injustice, whether against some form of tyranny at home
or against some perceived threat from abroad. Less familiar is
the symbolic violence of those who engage in conflict with techniques which they, at least, perceive to be nonviolent. And more
puzzling is the behavior of others who demonstrate their hostility
through acts of destruction while, at the same time, they shout
slogans of "peace."

Some of the difficulties which entangle those who call for
change through acts of violence or symbolic violence can be rendered open to keener analysis by recognizing that almost all the
action is policy oriented: the character of means as they relate to
ends receives less and less consideration. A policy which is taken
to be unjust is readily attacked through any means available—
without regard for the effect of the means employed. The result
is familiar to those who have analyzed the central difficulty

which has beset, among others, the philosophical anarchist. For anarchism has taken as its prime objective the abolition of violence; yet anarchist activists have repeatedly resorted to violence in fruitless efforts to accomplish that objective. The anarchist dilemma faces those today who seek to bring about change without regard for the effect of the means employed and without concern for fashioning alternative programs and policies which could adequately be substituted for those which are to go down in the heat of battle. This problem of the relationship of ends to means has become increasingly acute. In grappling with it, I submit that there is something to be learned from contrasting commonly employed methods of agitation with another approach to action which I am calling here creative conflict.

As a point of departure I take the Gandhian technique known as satyagraha—a method poorly understood, rarely used, and therefore left unrefined and ill adapted to our times. In exploring the ways in which such a technique can be contrasted both to violence and to methods not violent or just short of violence we may discover the direction in which it is necessary to move if a method is ever to be designed whereby conflict can become truly creative on the contemporary scene.

CREATIVE CONFLICT

A distinguished Norwegian philosopher, Arne Naess, has formulated the following axiom: One ought to act in a group struggle in such a way that long-run hostility will be reduced to a minimum.[2] The well-known psychoanalyst Erik Erikson has also given us a basic rule: One ought to act in such a way that his opponent is allowed, or encouraged, to grow.[3] Both scholars abstracted these axioms from the Gandhian method of satyagraha. They touch upon aspects of this complex means of persuasion.

Further exploration yields this understanding: satyagraha is a means which potentially (a) embraces a method of inquiry, (b) uses pressure but contains it, (c) focuses upon problem-solving rather than problem-creating. It is essentially a method for effecting change, and, when applied rigorously, it safeguards, and does not threaten, basic values. Though it may well be used to bring about change in established institutions, it is a technique which strengthens, and does not destroy, those institutions through which basic values can be applied and preserved.

The objective of satyagraha is the constructive transforming of relationships in a manner which not only effects a change (such as a change of policy) but also assures the restructuring of the situation which led to conflict. This calls for a modification of attitudes and requires fulfillment of the significant needs of all parties originally in conflict. The Gandhian method does not allow for overwhelming the opponent or even for the total destruction of his position. Simply to inveigh against an opponent as "incorrect" or "morally wrong" without engaging in extensive efforts of constructive persuasion is to deny the creative potential of satyagraha.

What is said below about the dynamics involved in satyagraha is a formulation of an ideal approach to creative conflict, the understanding of which could illuminate for those who genuinely seek constructive solutions the manner in which it is possible to establish mutually acceptable advance between and among parties involved in conflict. No implication is intended here that satyagraha, even as employed by Gandhi, always lived up to its potential. But for those who would employ such a technique and continue, as did Gandhi, to experiment with its refinement, there is the promise that as a result of their experience in endeavoring to apply the method in bringing about change they will find that they too will change. Creative conflict of the order examined here demands of its leaders the expectation and readiness to change subjectively as well as to effect and deal with changes in the objectives for which the technique is undertaken. This is among the most significant discoveries issuing from Gandhi's leadership.[4]

THE DYNAMICS OF CREATIVE CONFLICT

In common with other forms of social action to effect change, satyagraha uses pressure. But in the Gandhian technique pressure, in the sense of a force acting against some opposing force (to adopt a mechanical meaning of the term), describes only the initial action in a complex system of dynamics. The satyagrahi (one who uses satyagraha) develops an interacting force with the opponent to produce a new movement in order to change the direction or even the content of the force thus generated. The opponent is engaged in a manner intended to transform the relationships into a form or pattern which could not earlier have been predicted with any precision. The subtleties of response from the opponent are channeled back into the satyagrahi's movement and these responding pressures are given the maximum opportunity to influence subsequent procedures, and even the content of the satyagrahi's own claims and objectives.[5]

In contrast to the above process, the common use of pressure in campaigns of social protest is one of steady pushing or thrusting, and it usually results in distress and often in destruction. Pressure in this sense does not allow for the acceptance or reflection of influences from the opposition. The strike is typical of this straightforward application of pressure. It is commonly used to impose an economic burden and is intended to hurt business or to strain relationships so that normal functions are brought to a halt, or at least inhibited. Normal functioning cannot be resumed until policy changes are instituted or demands granted. In contrast, satyagraha sets out to develop alternatives which antagonists on all sides can accept.

An imaginative approach to devising techniques adapted to given instances of conflict is essential in satyagraha; it is, in fact, an inherent part of the philosophy which underlies the Gandhian method. It can be likened to the process of inquiry and solution of problems described by John Dewey in his analysis of purposive action involved in the thought process. One who successfully seeks to learn approaches a problem with certain purposes. And as he comes into contact with fact, those purposes are changed; they may be modified and they are almost certainly enriched. New elements will be perceived and that perception will, in its turn, modify the purposes which were brought to the situation. The inquirer's perspective is continually developed and he moves toward creative solutions which were not available to him in his initial approach to the problem. His first purposes and interests served to guide his inquiry, but what he comes to learn when in contact with the facts guides the further development of his purposes and interests. In some sense his initial approach is blind, for his facts are limited; yet he must start from what he already knows. In creative conflict, as in the process of purposive action in the thought process, the important thing is that one can learn and that in the course of learning one's initial purposes may well broaden and become more profound.

In place of the harassment and distress so commonly issuing from contemporary efforts to effect change through active protest, satyagraha insists upon a fundamentally supportive approach. As the satyagrahi moves to bring about change in a given situation through persuading his opponent to modify or alter the position under attack, he seeks to strengthen interpersonal relationships and intrapersonal satisfactions. He does this through acts of support and, where appropriate, through service to the opponent. Such an approach is based upon a psychologically sound understanding of suffering and the capacity of man to change.

If one seriously engages in introspection, he can readily come to understand that fundamental change of a profound order is indeed accompanied by suffering. The more rigid and fixed the attitude, or the more habitual the behavior, the more painful is the experience and process of change. Persisting, obstinate attitudes are not without their cause. They perform a function which has its origin in personal history. They are part of an intrapersonal economy, any disruption of which will be experienced as distress and even as a major personal threat. It follows from these elementary psychological facts that change can best be effected in the context of reassurance and through efforts to limit the area of attack. It may well be impossible to bring about a change in attitudes and to achieve the transformation of relationships without extensive reassurance and support. Otherwise, the conflict becomes exacerbated, the opposition hardened, and the prospects of a life-and-death struggle enhanced. When change of a fundamental nature is involved, the harassment of a strike or demonstration will not achieve the response desired—

or if it does achieve a change it will be through overwhelming the opponent and destroying the possibility of a sound, transformed relationship. In satyagraha, the more serious the expected change—and therefore the more radical the destruction of established patterns—the more essential it is to undertake counter and parallel constructive efforts of a high order.

The creative process called for is, then, one which can be applied in a supportive style toward a restructured end. This integrative mode of approach does not depend upon optimistic notions that mankind is essentially and necessarily good; it is, rather, based upon the knowledge of the psychological needs common to us all.

THE NATURE OF SYMBOLIC VIOLENCE

The destructive effects of violence are widely recognized, and it is readily conceded that these effects extend beyond the physical. Violence once-removed, through unconscious symbolization, and acted upon in ways which exclude the cruder physical forms of destruction, may indeed be more treacherous than frank and open violence.

The use of symbol, if the results are to be understood, let alone controlled, requires a high degree of awareness. Those who consciously set out to apply symbolic violence have a better chance of control and effectiveness than those who proceed with forms of social protest or passive resistance without the recognition that they are involved in violence once-removed. It is for this reason that the leader who would organize a movement without violence should be pressed to understand his techniques and to explore his strategies.

"Symbolic" pertains to something that denotes or stands for something else. The distinction should be made between that which stands for something else because it has been consciously given a conventional or contrived significance and that which represents an unconscious wish. (The unconscious wish may be to act violently, or it may be a counterdesire, i.e., to be nonviolent, or it may even be both at the same time.) Those who consciously set out with nonviolent intent and destructive objective to prosecute their action through means which are physically violent may be said to engage in symbolic violence in the first sense: their nonviolent acts have the contrived significance of violence once-removed. Those who, on the other hand, are attached to the ideals of nonviolence while, at the same time, they unwittingly engage in destructive acts, may be involved in symbolic violence described in the second meaning of "symbolic."

The individual who uses symbolic violence but who believes that he is using nonviolence may be unaware of the substitute nature of his behavior, which, in its unconscious meaning, is violent and destructive. The behavior of those who consciously contrive to use symbolic violence, as well as of those who believe their actions to be free from violence, may both be substitutive in nature. The manner in which the guilt of others is used to promote a "nonviolent" movement can be understood by applying the second meaning of "symbolic."

Some social and political activists set out to disclose the guilt of their chosen opponents and to use this disclosure as a technique in prosecuting their efforts to effect change even though their action may be put forward as nonviolent. The use of guilt and guilt disclosure is sometimes dictated by a consideration indirectly related to the given conflict, as, for example, a commitment to an ideological position not germane to the conflict at hand. (Such a commitment is that of the ideologue to the doctrine of class warfare.) Others claim moral superiority, but their conviction of such superiority may arise from their failure to examine personal motives or to appreciate their effect (and that of behavior based upon personal needs) in the objective circumstance. Whatever the intent, when a group is enjoined by its leaders to disclose guilt on the part of others—or, as in recent times, to insist that our society is guilty and therefore sick— while at the same time the action-oriented group sets about demonstrating its own guiltlessness, the mechanism suggests psychological projection. The true meaning of such an approach may well be an unconscious sense of guilt in the demonstrators—and perhaps in the leaders—themselves. It may even reflect unconscious guilt on the part of the activist against the very persons upon whose behalf he is engaged in social action. Producing a sense of guilt in others is destined to exacerbate the conflict. This may, of course, be its intent—and certainly in uncomplicated situations it might achieve its purpose. But where extensive and fundamental change is desired, reliance upon such a procedure will fail to achieve any clear and constructive purpose. For guilt is a destructive force and is closely related to fear and hatred and violence.

The point to be made here is not that the self-righteous demonstrator may himself harbor guilt, but rather that he may well be *unaware* of his own feelings of guilt. The freely informed and acutely aware individual does not point the finger of shame at others. He sets about his task in quite different ways. And in recognizing his own prejudices—wherever they may lie—he engages with his companions and enters into the struggle with his opponents in order to search for constructive solutions and to transform relationships. Gandhi repeatedly warned of the dangers involved in focusing upon the misdeeds of the opponent. "After all," he observed, "no one is wicked by nature . . . and if others are wicked, are we the less so? That attitude is inherent in satyagraha." Earlier, Gandhi had written, "Whenever I see an erring man, I say to myself, I have also erred," and again, in opposing the use of forms of passive resistance, he insisted, "We must refrain from crying 'shame, shame' to anybody; we must not use any coercion to persuade other people to adopt our way. We must guarantee to them the same freedom we claim for ourselves."

Among the most demanding tasks for the satyagrahi is that of extending areas of rationality. The significance of the irrational must be given full recognition, but, at the same time, it is essential to refrain from using irrational elements in an emotional appeal to onlookers and opponents in an effort to gain adherents without an explication of the nature of the conflict and the issues for which solutions are genuinely sought.

SELF-RIGHTEOUSNESS AND RESPONSIBILITY

If change is to be sought nonviolently it is incumbent upon the activist to concern himself with the problems he is presenting to his opponent. The relationship to those one seeks to change calls for a high level of responsibility. A recognition of the burden his demands place upon others may well prove crucial. The activist is expecting his opponent to reject patterns of behavior to which the opponent has long been accustomed—behavior which may well appear to him to be justified and even to accord with high moral standards. If conventional social forms are involved which carry sanctions for failure to comply (as in the law or established custom) the demonstrator, by his act of contravention, is presenting to the opponent and to third parties formerly not involved in the conflict the necessity to make a conscious choice. This choice requires the opponent to have faith in the demonstrator's judgment. For the demonstrator is stating a position contrary to hitherto accepted form and usage. He is saying, in effect, "The established conventions and authorities are wrong; what I am doing is right: accept my way."

The well-launched demonstration is, then, calculated to confront the opponent in such a manner that he is forced to make a choice. Opponents and otherwise uninvolved onlookers are faced with the need to examine their own behavior. Conduct which was formerly taken for granted is in this way questioned. If the opponent and the onlooker persist in the old way, the behavior which had been habitual and automatic now becomes conscious and for that very reason it is likely to gain the strength of conviction. It is out of such a system of dynamics that counterrevolutions arise. They are unwittingly encouraged by those who do not have adequate methods and alternative objectives.

The responsibility for forcing a choice does, indeed, require serious consideration and study. Questions should be raised about one's justification in asking an opponent to trust this new judgment which is alien and unwelcome. When responsibility of this order is carefully weighed, the need for actions of support to the opponent can more clearly be understood. The details of supportive action and the manner in which it may be undertaken can best emerge in the course of pursuing a satyagraha-type struggle where the extent of responsibility is examined within the context of that specific conflict situation. When conscious decision is forced upon others, it becomes all the more important that guilt be dispelled, fear abated, and passions controlled.

The forcing of new choices is a tactic for effecting change in a static situation. At the critical juncture when choice is forced, the satyagrahi must shoulder his greatest burdens. He will be confronted by persons seized with doubts and uncertainties, and it is his obligation to tolerate their abuse, should it be offered, and to find ways in which to strengthen and reassure his opponents. His own strength at such junctures is put to the greatest test, and his own capacity for creative thought and imaginative act is taxed to the fullest.

As the satyagrahi engages his opponent in constructive conflict, his responsibility is to be understood also in terms of responsiveness. It is of the essence of satyagraha that every response from the opponent be accepted as genuine and that all undertakings or countersuggestions of the opponent be considered to have been given in good faith. This is not only a matter of strategy, based upon an active search for truth, but it is also an effective tactic. If the opponent gives any indication of changing his position and altering his behavior—in either direction—this indication must be given full recognition. It is essential to accept, as genuine, threats of violence or acts of hostility as well as any expression of intent on the part of the opponent to move toward a resolution of the conflict. To demonstrate acceptance and belief in the opponent's good faith will serve to hold him to his word, to diminish his hesitation, and to encourage the realization of his perhaps shaky intent.

One characteristic of contemporary social protest movements is the readiness with which their proponents deride every move made by those they oppose. They are quick to believe that the opposition is acting in bad faith. This readiness to doubt the

good faith of an opponent may be put forward as a piece of so-
phistication based upon experience or knowledge of human nature. In operation such an approach is poor strategy and worse
tactics.[6] By contrast, the satyagrahi's move to credit the opponent with genuine intent requires the capacity to tolerate abuse
(as in instances where the opponent has, in fact, acted in bad
faith) and to exercise forbearance. Gandhi once said that "impa-
tience is a phase of violence." Symbolic violence does, indeed,
take many forms, and of all forms of violence it is the most difficult to understand. To acquire an adequate appreciation of its
dangers demands persistent effort and keen analysis.

What Remains to Be Done?

Once the limitations of symbolic violence (as well as of violence) have been recognized, and when conventional nonviolence
has been tried and found wanting, the question then arises:
What, indeed, can be done to establish alternative methods of
conducting conflict? I have already suggested that we learn more
from historical examples of the use of satyagraha. But that
places us in a different period, reviewing situations which, although instructive, have a limited bearing upon our present predicament. Satyagraha—even in its formulation as an ideal type
—is only a beginning. It remains for us to seek out the refinements in technique and to explore the ways in which creative
conflict can be made a concrete strategy for the use of those who
seek to effect fundamental changes both on the domestic scene
and in international conflict.[7]

My underlying assumption is that conflict is inevitable and
that man must develop the means to conduct it with a minimum
of destruction. To date, few efforts along these lines have been
made—and they have stumbled over artificial blocks. First we
must ask the pertinent questions; then it is imperative that we
press ahead toward the designing of techniques worthy of man's
genius. The challenge is clear: violence, nonviolence, and symbolic violence are simply not enough. Gandhian satyagraha has

pointed the way out of some of our difficulties. Surely mankind is not so bankrupt in ideas that we cannot apply what is already known to the sort of inquiry which can lead to techniques equal to the challenge. The need for alternatives is evident and the task is surely the most urgent which man has ever faced.

NOTES

1. For a statement of "permanent revolution" as a characteristic of democratic countries see Carl J. Friedrich, "An Introductory Note on Revolution," in *Revolution* (Nomos VIII), ed. Carl J. Friedrich (New York: Atherton, 1966), p. 4.
2. See his article, "A Systematization of Gandhian Ethics of Conflict Resolution," *The Journal of Conflict Resolution,* II, no. 2 (June 1958).
3. See Erik H. Erikson, *Insight and Responsibility* (New York: W. W. Norton, 1964), chap. 6, "The Golden Rule in the Light of New Insight."
4. For an elaboration of this theme, see Joan V. Bondurant, "The Non-conventional Political Leader in India," in *Leadership and Political Institutions in India,* ed. Richard L. Park and Irene Tinker, (Princeton, N. J.: Princeton University Press, 1959).
5. This process has been described as the "Gandhian dialectic" in Joan V. Bondurant, *Conquest of Violence: The Gandhian Philosophy of Conflict,* rev. ed. (Berkeley: University of California Press, 1967). See this work also for detailed historical examples of how satyagraha was used in India during the Gandhi era.
6. It is this aspect of simple passive resistance—in contradistinction to satyagraha—which accounts for the frequent failures of passive resisters.
7. For an elaboration upon these points see Portia Bell Hume and Joan V. Bondurant, "The Significance of Unasked Questions in the Study of Conflict," *Inquiry* (University of Oslo, Fall 1964), pp. 318–327. See also Joan V. Bondurant, "Paraguerrilla Strategy: A New Concept in Arms Control," in *Weapons Management and World Politics,* ed. J. David Singer, joint issue of the *Journal of Conflict Resolution,* 7:3 (September 1963), 235–245, and the *Journal of Arms Control,* 1:4 (October 1963), 329–339.

IV

Is There an Alternative to Violence?

9

Fractionating Conflict

ROGER FISHER

This paper is not concerned with debating whether major conflicts of interest exist between countries; it is concerned with dealing with them. It does not suggest that any one country has complete control over the formulation of international conflict issues but that each country has a measure of control. It does not suggest that it is always wise to fractionate conflict into little issues but that it is often wise to do so. Actions affecting the size of an issue should be undertaken consciously, with the advantages and disadvantages in mind. Little study has been devoted to the criteria and methods by which a country should formulate and expand or contract issues in controversy. Arms are used only over issues. Perhaps more important than the field of arms control is the field of "issue control."

From *Daedalus* (Summer 1964), "Population, Prediction, Conflict, Existentialism," pp. 920–941. Copyright 1964 by the American Academy of Arts and Sciences. Reprinted (abridged) by permission of the publisher. *Author's note:* This article is a version of a chapter from *International Conflict and Behavioral Science: The Craigville Papers,* published by Basic Books, Inc., in June 1964. This volume grew out of the American Academy of Arts and Sciences Conference, "Alternative Ways of Handling Conflict: Behavioral Science Research Toward Peace," held in Craigville, Cape Cod.

The way in which a country wishes to carry on a dispute must be judged in light of the nation's objectives. The United States' basic objectives are: first, to win each dispute with another country, and second, to avoid war and develop a fair way of settling such disputes—objectives which are somewhat inconsistent. While the United States would like to win *each* dispute, it is not seeking a world in which any one country wins *every* dispute. Internationally as well as domestically, our government is simultaneously interested in winning each case and in promoting the rule of law—a regime in which the government does not always win. It is interested in winning disputes and in settling them peacefully. No absolute priority can be established between these two objectives; both need to be kept in mind in each dispute. It is against these objectives that the process of formulating and fractionating conflict issues must be judged.

There are, perhaps, an infinite number of ways in which international issues might be sliced. For a first approximation, it may be useful to consider five dimensions which measure the size of a conflict issue:

1. The parties on each side of the issue
2. The immediate physical issue involved
3. The immediate issue of principle
4. The substantive precedent which settlement will establish
5. The procedural precedent which settlement will establish.

With respect to each of these, there is a certain amount of choice as to how big or small the issue is made. Although these variables are not wholly independent, they will serve as a basis for exploring different ways in which conflict issues may be increased or decreased in size.

PARTIES ON EACH SIDE OF THE ISSUE

In traditional international law, the nation is considered as the proper unit to represent the interests of a citizen who is injured. In some circumstances, the nation is held responsible for wrongs committed by its citizens.

Disputes between people ruled by different governments need not be treated as intergovernmental disputes. Disputes between groups in different states within the United States are rarely treated as interstate disputes. Among nations, even actions by government officials are often deliberately treated as though the government itself were not involved.

There are advantages in downgrading a dispute and in treating it as one between individuals, or at least as one in which the other government is not involved. As long as disputes are considered in this way, there is little chance of war.

Treating disputes as cases between individuals or groups rather than nations has the further virtue of establishing cross-cutting conflicts. In such conflicts, the opponents in one controversy are not identical with the opponents in another. On the international scene today, Yugoslavia and Poland have helped this country understand that our disputes with the Soviet Union and our disputes with communism are not always the same thing. By identifying more accurately our opponent in certain Far East situations as "China" rather than as "communism," we may find that we have reduced the size of our opponent and also that on occasion we have an ally in the Soviet Union.

There are often, however, conveniences in treating a single government as the responsible opponent in what would otherwise be a mass of unrelated problems. A simple overall solution may be possible only by considering matters on a government-to-government basis. Using one dispute as leverage on another, as discussed below, often requires a preliminary step—that of treating as governmental two disputes which otherwise would be considered to involve different groups or individuals.

Defining the parties to a dispute is thus a basic way of making disputes bigger or smaller.

IMMEDIATE PHYSICAL ISSUE INVOLVED

Any particular conflict can be thought of as having a certain minimum size in factual or physical terms. This is measured by the inconsistency between the physical events desired by the two adversaries.

There are two ways of expanding the physical size of an issue: first, by defining more broadly the subject matter in dispute; second, by bringing in different subjects which are related only because the parties are the same.

It seems clear that if a subject is too narrowly defined, there will be little possibility of a bargain. The narrower the point, the more likely it is that a change will benefit one party only. It would seem desirable to expand the subject until it is large enough for a bargain which benefits each, if not to the same extent, at least to some degree. As a general rule, enlargement of the issue beyond that point is unwise.

The immediate issue under discussion between two sides may be expanded by coupling one dispute with another. Here the connection is made not by broadening the definition of the subject matter but by recognizing that two matters involve the same parties. The considerations involved in coupling one dispute with another deserve more study. If the joining of problems is made as an offer, the process seems constructive, facilitating agreement: "I will let you have what you want in the X dispute if you will let me have what I want in the Y dispute." Coupling disputes in this way may increase the chances of agreement.

Even here, however, shifting the nature of the dispute—from a narrow subject matter to one in which the only common denominator is the parties involved—tends to bring up all possible issues in the relationship and may do more harm than good. It encourages the unfortunate "overall confrontation" described earlier. The joining of issues as leverage or bargaining currency, even when constructively looking toward a negotiated agreement, tends to shift the focus away from the merits of a problem and to put relative bargaining power in issue.

One way to improve the relationship between two adversaries may be to treat different subjects as separate issues. At roughly every other stage in the escalating process, each party has that option and should be aware of it.

It seems important to distinguish talking about an additional issue by way of a counteroffer, as discussed above, from taking action on an otherwise unrelated matter by way of pressure. When pressure produces counterpressure, the escalating process is much like that by which limited hostilities grow into all-out war. As is the case with limited war, the more unrelated the action of one country is to the action taken by the other, the more difficult it is to find a boundary to the conflict.

To be strong and effective, a country apparently needs principles and needs to adhere to them. Principles can be flexible, however, and the extent to which they are involved in a particular controversy can be limited in two ways. The first is by recognizing that we can be loyal to our principles without insisting that our opponents be disloyal to theirs. To arouse the maximum support of our own people, we often identify a dispute as a conflict of principle, in which one principle or the other must yield. We do this also as a form of committal strategy in which we strengthen our negotiating position by tying our own hands and making it harder to back down. If we wish to win a controversy, it would seem wiser to say that the solution we seek is not only consistent with our principles but is also consistent with those of our adversary—at least if properly construed and applied. By insisting that our adversary can come along without abandoning his principles, we make it easier for him to do so. In this way a country can remove an issue of principle from a controversy without in any sense abandoning its principles. If another country is prepared to accept a physical solution which we regard as consistent with our principles, no principle of ours requires that it first accept some generalized statement of what it is doing.

The second way of limiting the extent to which principle is involved in a controversy is to recognize the difference between principle and the application of principle. In almost every dispute, there are conflicting principles involved. In a lawsuit, each side urges that a different principle should be the controlling one. Litigation may simply determine that, in this case, the principle does not properly apply. The same determination can be reached through negotiation; to do so is not to be disloyal to principle.

Recognizing where possible that a dispute involves a question of the *application* of principle rather than the central principle itself should make it possible to decrease the stakes. Nonetheless, in every controversy, a certain minimum amount of principle is involved. The size of a controversy may be measured in terms of both the substantive and procedural precedents which its resolution will set.

SUBSTANTIVE PRECEDENT WHICH SETTLEMENT WOULD ESTABLISH

In almost every conflict each side is thinking not only of how much it would lose immediately if it yielded a point but also of how much it would lose by way of precedent. The impact of a precedent depends upon its *strength* and its *scope*. To the extent that these can be controlled, the size of the matter in conflict can be changed.

The scope of a precedent is always somewhat ambiguous. In political affairs, as in the legal system, ambiguity permits a nice accommodation between consistency and flexibility as new circumstances arise. The minimum scope of a precedent is determined by that which cannot reasonably be distinguished from it. Additional scope may be established by what is said before and during the resolution of an issue. The language used by one or both sides may turn a simple case into a test case. Significant possibilities exist for limiting the size of a conflict by limiting the precedent. If the parties agree that a controversy is a test case which will decide a broad category of issues, the scope of the precedent is thereby enlarged.

PROCEDURAL PRECEDENT WHICH SETTLEMENT WOULD ESTABLISH

A close relationship exists between the substantive issue involved and the procedural precedent established by reaching an agreement. To the extent that a settlement is substantively sound, it can be justified "on its merits"; the fact that concessions were made will have limited effect. If both parties have made some concessions, the effects are likely to be in balance. If one party has made all the concessions, the Munich situation obtains. The effects of such a concession need to be examined in terms of their influence on each party and on third states. The lessons learned from Munich deserve more study than they have received.

The first lesson—that a country may not succeed in pacifying another by yielding to its purportedly last demands—has been thoroughly absorbed. In fact, appeasement has become such a bad word that there is little attempt to identify situations in which it might be politically effective.

The second lesson of Munich is that the party to whom the concession has been given may think that a procedural precedent has been established and may seek further concessions in the same way. Having discovered that the British would not fight over one issue, Hitler apparently assumed that they would not fight over a comparable issue. Third states may have reached the same conclusion.

The third lesson of Munich, however, is that Hitler was wrong. Governments, like individuals, are tolerant to a degree. They will cooperate with others on a give-and-take basis, but unless concessions are reciprocal, it is less likely, rather than more, that additional concessions will be made. Of course, if a country gives up territory or arms of substantive importance, it may become weaker through concessions. The Munich example, however, suggests that the effect of a procedural precedent on a country that yields has been widely exaggerated. It suggests that the famous "slippery slope" goes uphill, not down.

FRACTIONATION OF DISPUTES

When considering only the "procedural" objective of the United States—to avoid war and to improve the method of settling international differences—it appears that the practice of fractionating conflict issues is definitely to our interest. Separating issues into their smallest components and dealing with them one at a time reduces the risk of war significantly.

Fractionating conflict should avoid the stalemate that comes from a nation-to-nation confrontation in which neither country feels that it can make any concession without losing part of an overall war. To the extent that issues are decided separately, there is an increased chance that they are decided on their merits, that is, in light of their particular facts and circumstances. In this sense, agreements reached might be objectively better. Piecemeal settlement also recognizes that everything cannot be done at once and permits progress in certain areas while other matters are being worked out.

No general statement, of course, can be made that either fractionating a conflict issue or enlarging it will always be better for a country from the point of view of winning the matter in dispute.

Coupling one issue with another may be useful as a form of pressure. If one country has sufficient power for effective arm twisting, the desired substantive result may be accomplished. Such substantive gain must be weighed against the procedural loss which deciding disputes on the basis of superior power involves. There are other limitations on the pressure technique. When dealing with an opponent who has the opportunity to escalate a conflict issue by throwing in counterleverage and counterthreats, the tactic can backfire.

Even when one country of superior power is applying pressure in large quantities, the effectiveness of that pressure is likely to depend upon keeping the issue on which it is focused small. The effectiveness of pressure is increased by keeping the objective narrow and making it easy for the adversary to back down.

The coupling technique may also be a useful way of winning one dispute at the expense of another. If an issue that is likely to be lost anyway is on the table, a country may be able to retrieve something by coupling that dispute with one on which the adversary might yield. If an issue that a country strongly desires to win is on the table, perhaps it can be bought by coupling it with a "loser."

Similarly, expanding the subject matter under dispute may make it possible to work out an agreement in which we win something. Negotiating the allocation of a single radio frequency between several countries would be difficult. There would be more likelihood of success if the subject were broadened to include enough frequencies so that each country would get at least one. Finally, if it is already clear that one side is going to win in a particular conflict situation, the larger the terms in which the issue can be defined, the more that side will win.

These instances indicate that fractionating a conflict situation —insisting that the issues be dealt with separately and in their narrowest possible scope—may not always be the wisest strategy. However, they do not cover the most frequent occasions on which countries tend to insist that big issues are involved.

ESCALATION OF ISSUES

Perhaps the most important proposition developed in this preliminary consideration of the field of issue control is that a country which defines an issue in large terms has adopted a negative strategy. An issue is often defined broadly as a deliberate defensive maneuver. Rather than treat the transit of men and materials from West Germany to West Berlin as a group of narrow, pragmatic questions, the United States has defined the problem in terms of freedom versus communism. The West has insisted that any interference with its access to Berlin would be serious enough to justify a war—including, perhaps, a nuclear war.

Insisting that a small change from the status quo would bring disastrous consequences is a defensive move, a kind of rearguard action, slowing down the pace of change. It retards the loss of a substantive point, but it is unlikely to be wholly successful in preserving the status quo. The United States can insist that any interference with our right of access to Berlin will be viewed as grounds for war. This may slow down the slice-by-slice "salami tactics" of the Soviet Union, but it can hardly stop them. To insist that a small change would be a justification for war does not by itself make it so. If the slices are thin enough and are taken slowly enough, the prophesied doom does not in fact materialize. The country which defines small issues and presses forward on them is likely to make headway which its adversary, by insisting that large principles are at stake, may delay but be unable to stop.

If increasing the size of an issue has little long-run promise as a defensive strategy, it has even less promise as an offensive technique. If a party desires to alter the status quo, defining an issue as one involving a large subject matter or big principles tends to make success less likely. Almost inevitably, change from the status quo must be brought about incrementally. Even those who have the power to bring about major changes and would like to do so must face the question of where to begin. If one is to be effective in domestic politics, he must combine the public support which broad issues and principles can arouse with the pursuit of narrowly defined goals.

It would seem equally important for a government which wishes to alter the behavior of another government to define its immediate goal in narrow and specific terms, to break up the big issues into smaller ones, and to press for these separately. The British experience in seeking to "topple Nasser" is instructive. By defining an issue in all-or-nothing terms, we tend to make sure that we get nothing unless we are prepared to exert the force required to get all. Having declared that the choice is between communism and freedom, little victories look like compromises with communism. In this context it is difficult for us to apply the "salami tactics" of moving forward slice by slice.

Escalating a matter into a large issue of principle appears to be somewhat effective as a defensive strategy; at least it can gain time. It would seem generally unwise as a strategy to pursue in areas in which we would like to change the status quo. Fractionating issues, on the other hand, seems almost invariably the best tactic for a country seeking to bring about change.

Conclusions

Internationally, it is more difficult to force a decision on the little issues. The lack of compulsory jurisdiction for the International Court of Justice means that we have no institutionalized method of bringing up and disposing of one case at a time. The virtues of adopting and pressing for a small specific objective, however, go far beyond the legal machinery. In international politics as in domestic politics, the strategy of separating out small and immediate issues and dealing with them one at a time would seem likely to advance our social and substantive goals.

If the United States continues to press, in the United Nations and elsewhere, on many small and separate issues—issues in which our position makes more practical sense than the position of our opponents—we have a fair chance of prevailing.

Fractionating conflict would thus seem to be a promising strategy not only for reducing the risk of war but also for promoting victory for our values. This does not mean that such a strategy is opposed to the real interests of any other country. As we need to be reminded so often, the world is not a zero-sum game where victory for some automatically means defeat for others. As long, however, as most issues are dealt with in terms of a nation-to-nation conflict, common interests will be lost in the major conflict which precludes agreement. It would seem that only by dividing up the issues and considering them separately in small units will we be able to find and to work together in those areas where we have common goals and common interests, and thus obtain the optimum accommodation possible.

10

Comments on "Fractionating Conflict"

LAWRENCE S. FINKELSTEIN

A "response" to an article, even a solicited one, is bound to emphasize its differences with the article being responded to, and to slight the points of agreement which remain unexpressed. Let it be explicit then. Roger Fisher is right in urging us to be concerned with "issue control." He provokes us constructively and with imagination. Reading his article was, for this critic, a learning experience. Moreover, overall, the article elicited more agreement with its insights than disagreement.

Yet, the article, although it employs examples, treats conflict as an abstract concept in a way which leaves one wondering to

From *Daedalus* (Summer 1964), "Population, Prediction, Conflict, Existentialism," pp. 942–945. Copyright 1964 by the American Academy of Arts and Sciences. Reprinted (abridged) by permission of the publisher.

what extent the abstraction resembles the reality to which the prescriptions are supposed to apply. Conflicts between states, after all, involve the interaction of values, the perceptions and understandings of the actors, the means by which the conflicts are conducted, the international political environment in which they occur, and the political processes and human relationships which affect the decisions of governmental leaders. The possibilities for variation among conflicts are virtually infinite. To treat them as if they are easily summed up in the one word "conflict" is not to clarify the subject very significantly. Of course, abstraction for the purpose of model building in social research is a useful, indeed necessary, technique. Presumably, "economic man" no more resembled the complex realities it helped to analyze than the Fisher model of conflict resembles the complex and varied phenomena it seeks to synthesize for the purpose of the analysis. Perhaps, like the economists, Professor Fisher can be induced to carry this beginning further—to reconstruct his skeletal model of conflict on the basis of materials drawn from life, and to test and draw conclusions from the hypotheses with which his article presents us. After the process is complete, and a book has been written, a condensation or synopsis in article form would be well worth reading.

If Professor Fisher takes this advice, one question which deserves clarification is whether there is a distinction between issues and conflicts. Professor Fisher does not explicitly equate the two, but gives them the same weight in his analysis, seems to reach conclusions about them based on the assumption that they are identical, and fails to examine the factors that differentiate them as they affect his theses. To point up the distinction, one could, speciously perhaps, argue that issues are potential sources of conflict which can be resolved by following Professor Fisher's guidelines, while conflicts are those more intractable disputes which defy such attempts at resolution.

Clearly, Professor Fisher offers wise advice when he urges that it is important to be alert to choices in defining issues which affect the risk that they will become acute conflicts which resist settlement. In this context, his questions and prescriptions are sensitive, interesting, and valuable, even if they are not always entirely persuasive. Thus, he urges, for example, that individuals, rather than governments, can sometimes be considered the parties to disputes. However, many disputes transcending national boundaries do ordinarily occur between individuals and remain at that level. A body of law—private international law or conflict of laws—exists to deal with such situations. Moreover, international law establishes standards—denial of justice and exhaustion of local remedies, for example—by which private disputes can become governmental ones. Disputes which have become governmental disputes have often become so either because they meet these standards or because they are intrinsically governmental in character. It is hard to argue successfully that issues involving countries that have no private enterprise are very likely to remain nongovernmental ones.

Professor Fisher's operating assumption appears to be that what he describes as the "sizing" of disputes or conflicts is a matter which can often be determined by rational choice. Again, it is useful to be reminded that we should be alert to such choices when it is possible to make them. However, it seems reasonable to ask how often one should expect to be able to make such choices with respect to intense conflict situations. His assumption is that the components of a dispute—the parties, the immediate physical issues, the principles at stake and the way they are applied, and the precedential implications—although inherently connected, can be treated separately. It is far from clear that this is so in all cases. For example, the Fisher assumption does not seem to respond with sufficient candor to the difference which he recognizes between conflicts which consist of accumulated grievances over discrete issues which *are* separable, and conflicts which exist because of fundamental hostility arising out of ultimately conflicting objectives and principles. In the latter category, issues may be no more than the means by which conflict is conducted. If the relations between the parties resemble *ad hominem* arguments, it is because the parties' beliefs about their intentions toward each other lie at the heart of the matter.

Even in such conflicts one should, of course, be alert to the possibility that disputes over issues can be insulated or separated from the main source of overriding conflict. It was, after all, possible to reach agreement on an Austrian peace treaty, an Antarctic disarmament treaty, and, most recently, on a reduction in production of nuclear materials, even though these issues and others on which agreement has been possible were intimately related to the overall texture of relationships between the Soviet Union and the United States. With respect to even such successes, however, it may be an instructive rather than merely a semantic distinction to point out that the settlement of these issues did not take place apart from, but rather as part of, the conduct of conflict relationships between the parties.

Professor Fisher, whether he focuses on the settlement of conflicts or the conduct of conflicts, concentrates his attention on the procedures without reference to the substance of issues or to the sharing of the values in dispute between the disputants. How the issues come out is, obviously, important and not only because of the interest each side in a dispute has in winning it. The question whether a particular solution is viable is an important criterion of whether a dispute should be settled or not. For one thing, nonviable solutions, we have too often learned, may brew greater conflicts subsequently. The Versailles Treaty is a case in point, and our recent experience in Cyprus may prove to be another. Moreover, where conflicts involve the clash of conflicting value systems, the component issues which may appear to be separable nevertheless have to be examined in terms of the bearing they may have on the larger values in dispute.

Clearly, it would be wrong to suggest that basically hostile relationships are immutable. However, it is hard to believe that fundamental changes can be produced by Professor Fisher's method. In this connection, it would be worth examining what were the causes of such startling reversals of relationships as have occurred in recent memory, such as the conversion of Anglo-French enmity into alliance after Fashoda, the amelioration of Yugoslavia's postwar relationships with its neighbors, Germany's acceptance as a postwar friend of many of its wartime enemies, and the cordiality that has marked Japanese relations with the United States and its improving relations with neighboring countries in recent years. Merely to cite these examples is to suggest that such fundamental conversions seem historically to have come about as a result of forces other than the kind of chipping away at separable issues that Professor Fisher suggests. How much have Indian-Pakistan relations been fundamentally altered by the Indus waters settlement and all the other agreements, desirable in themselves, between the two countries? Is the amelioration of relations with the Soviet Union which we welcome today a consequence of the test ban treaty or is the latter a reflection of a mutual will to improve relations, growing from more fundamental causes rooted in changing perceptions of the relationship? One thing is clear: the role of the existing agreements between the Soviet Union and the United States as stepping stones on the path of improving relations is not separable from the larger context. The interaction between small issues and large conflicts is at the core of Professor Fisher's subject. It deserves thoughtful and intensive exploration.

All this brings me back to my starting point. Professor Fisher's argument is a valuable beginning, but one which needs and deserves fuller development, both from Professor Fisher and others who may be inspired to put his hypotheses to more elaborate tests than he has done in this article.

11

The Technique of Nonviolent Action

GENE SHARP

It is widely believed that military combat is the only effective means of struggle in a wide variety of situations of acute conflict. However, there is another whole approach to the waging of social and political conflict. Any proposed substitute for war in the defense of freedom must involve wielding power, confronting and engaging an invader's military might, and waging effective combat. The technique of nonviolent action, although relatively ignored and undeveloped, may be able to meet these requirements and provide the basis for a defense policy.

From *Civilian Resistance as a National Defense: Non-Violent Action against Aggression,* Adam Roberts, ed. (Harrisburg, Pa.: Stackpole Books, 1968), pp. 87–105. This book was also published in England under the title *The Strategy of Civilian Defence* (London: Faber and Faber Ltd., 1967). Reprinted (abridged) by permission of the editor and publishers.

ALTERNATIVE APPROACH TO THE CONTROL OF POLITICAL POWER

Military action is based largely on the idea that the most effective way of defeating an enemy is by inflicting heavy destruction on his armies, military equipment, transport system, factories, and cities. Weapons are designed to kill or destroy with maximum efficiency. Nonviolent action is based on a different approach: to deny the enemy the human assistance and cooperation which are necessary if he is to exercise control over the population. It is thus based on a more fundamental and sophisticated view of political power.

A ruler's power is ultimately dependent on support from the people he would rule. His moral authority, economic resources, transport system, government bureaucracy, army, and police—to name but a few immediate sources of his power—rest finally upon the cooperation and assistance of other people. If there is general conformity, the ruler is powerful.

But people do not always do what their rulers would like them to do. The factory manager recognizes this when he finds his workers leaving their jobs and machines, so that the production line ceases operation, or when he finds the workers persisting in doing something on the job which he has forbidden them to do. In many areas of social and political life comparable situations are commonplace. A man who has been a ruler and thought his power secure may discover that his subjects no longer believe he has any moral right to give them orders, that his laws are disobeyed, that the country's economy is paralyzed, that his soldiers and police are lax in carrying out repression or openly mutiny, and even that his bureaucracy no longer takes orders. When this happens, the man who has been ruler becomes simply another man, and his political power dissolves, just as the factory manager's power does when the workers no longer cooperate and obey. The equipment of his army may remain intact, his soldiers uninjured and very much alive, his cities unscathed, the factories and transport systems in full operational capacity, and the government buildings and offices unchanged. Yet because the human assistance which had created and supported his political power has been withdrawn, the former ruler finds that his political power has disintegrated.[1]

NONVIOLENT ACTION

The "technique" of "nonviolent action," which is based on this approach to the control of political power and the waging of political struggles, has been the subject of many misconceptions. For the sake of clarity the two terms are defined in this section.

The term *technique* is used here to describe the overall means of conducting an action or struggle. One can therefore speak of the technique of guerrilla warfare, of conventional warfare, and of parliamentary democracy.

The term *nonviolent action* refers to those methods of protest, noncooperation, and intervention in which the actionists, without employing physical violence, refuse to do certain things which they are expected, or required, to do, or do certain things which they are not expected, or are forbidden, to do. In a particular case there can of course be a combination of acts of omission and acts of commission.

Nonviolent action is a generic term; it includes the large class of phenomena variously called "nonviolent resistance," "satyagraha," "passive resistance," "positive action," and "nonviolent direct action." While it is not violent, it *is* action, and not inaction; passivity, submission, and cowardice must be surmounted if it is to be used. It is a means of conducting conflicts and waging struggles and is not to be equated with (though it may be accompanied by) purely verbal dissent or solely psychological influence. It is not "pacifism,"[2] and in fact has in the vast majority of cases been applied by nonpacifists. The motives for the adoption of nonviolent action may be religious or ethical, or they may be based on considerations of expediency. Nonviolent action is not an escapist approach to the problem of violence, for it can be applied in struggles against opponents relying on violent sanctions. The fact that in a conflict one side is nonviolent does not imply that the other side will also refrain from violence. Certain forms of nonviolent action may be regarded as efforts to persuade by action, while others are more coercive.

METHODS OF NONVIOLENT ACTION

There is a very wide range of methods, or forms, of nonviolent action, and at least 125 have been identified.[3] They fall into three classes—nonviolent protest, noncooperation, and nonviolent intervention.

Generally speaking, the methods of *nonviolent protest* are symbolic in their effect and produce an awareness of the existence of dissent. Under tyrannical regimes, however, where opposition is stifled, their impact can in some circumstances be very great. Methods of nonviolent protest include marches, pilgrimages, picketing, vigils, "haunting" officials, public meetings, issuing and distributing protest literature, renouncing honors, voluntary emigration, and humorous pranks.

The methods of *nonviolent noncooperation,* if sufficient numbers take part, are likely to present the opponent with difficulties in maintaining the normal efficiency and operation of the system, and in extreme cases the system itself may be threatened. Methods of nonviolent noncooperation include various types of strike (such as general strike, sit-down strike, industry strike, go-slow, and work-to-rule), various types of boycott (such as economic boycott, consumers' boycott, traders' boycott, rent refusal, international economic embargo, and social boycott), and various types of political noncooperation (such as boycott of government employment, boycott of elections, revenue refusal, civil disobedience, and mutiny).

The methods of *nonviolent intervention* have some features in common with the first two classes but also challenge the opponent more directly, and, assuming that fearlessness and discipline are maintained, relatively small numbers may have a disproportionately large impact. Methods of nonviolent intervention include sit-ins, fasts, reverse strikes, nonviolent obstruction, nonviolent invasion, and parallel government.

The exact way in which methods from each of the three classes are combined varies considerably from one situation to another. Generally speaking, the risks to the actionists on the one hand, and to the system against which they take action on the other, are least in the case of nonviolent protest and greatest in the case of nonviolent intervention. The methods of noncooperation tend to require the largest numbers but not to demand a large degree of special training from all participants. The methods of nonviolent intervention are generally effective if the participants possess a high degree of internal discipline and are willing to accept severe repression; the tactics must also be selected and carried out with particular care and intelligence.

Several important factors need to be considered in the selection of the methods to be used in a given situation. These factors include the type of issue involved, the nature of the opponent, his aims and strength, the type of counteraction he is likely to use, the depth of feeling both among the general population and among the likely actionists, the degree of repression the actionists are likely to be able to take, the general strategy of the overall campaign, and the amount of past experience and specific training the population and the actionists have had. Just as in military battle weapons are carefully selected, taking into account such factors as their range and effect, so also in nonviolent struggle the choice of specific methods is very important.

MECHANISMS OF CHANGE

In nonviolent struggles there are, broadly speaking, three mechanisms by which change is brought about. Usually there is a combination of the three. They are conversion, accommodation, and nonviolent coercion.

Conversion can be influenced by reason or argument, but in nonviolent action it is also likely to be influenced by emotional and moral factors, which can in turn be stimulated by the suffering of the nonviolent actionists, who seek to achieve their goals without inflicting injury on other people.

Accommodation as a mechanism of nonviolent action falls in an intermediary position between conversion and nonviolent coercion, and elements of both of the other mechanisms are generally involved. In accommodation, the opponent, although not converted, decides to grant the demands of the nonviolent actionists in a situation where he still has a choice of action. The social situation within which he must operate has been altered enough by nonviolent action to compel a change in his own response to the conflict, perhaps because he has begun to doubt the rightness of his position, perhaps because he does not think the matter worth the trouble caused by the struggle, and perhaps because he anticipates coerced defeat and wishes to accede gracefully or with a minimum of losses.

Nonviolent coercion may take place in any of three circumstances. Defiance may become too widespread and massive for the ruler to be able to control it by repression, the social and political system may become paralyzed, or the extent of defiance or disobedience among the ruler's own soldiers and other agents may undermine his capacity to apply repression. Nonviolent coercion becomes possible when those applying nonviolent action succeed in withholding, directly or indirectly, the necessary sources of the ruler's political power. His power then disintegrates, and he is no longer able to control the situation, even though he still wishes to do so.

Nonviolent Action versus Violence

There can be no presumption that an opponent, faced with an opposition relying solely on nonviolent methods, will suddenly renounce his capacity for violence. Instead, nonviolent action can operate against opponents able and willing to use violent sanctions and can counter their violence in such a way that they are thrown politically off balance in a kind of political *jiu-jitsu*.

Instead of confronting the opponent's police and troops with the same type of forces, nonviolent actionists counter these agents of the opponent's power indirectly. Their aim is to demonstrate that repression is incapable of cowing the populace and to deprive the opponent of his existing support, thereby undermining his ability or will to continue with the repression. Far from indicating the failure of nonviolent action, repression often helps to make clear the cruelty of the political system being opposed, and so to alienate support from it. Repression is often a kind of recognition from the opponent that the nonviolent action constitutes a serious threat to his policy or regime, one which he finds it necessary to combat.

Just as in war danger from enemy fire does not always force front line soldiers to panic and flee, so in nonviolent action repression does not necessarily produce submission. True, repression *may* be effective, but it may fail to halt defiance, and in this case the opponent will be in difficulties. Repression against a nonviolent group which persists in face of it and maintains nonviolent discipline may have the following effects: it may alienate the general population from the opponent's regime, making them more likely to join the resistance; it may alienate the opponent's usual supporters and agents, and their initial uneasiness may grow into internal opposition and at times into noncooperation and disobedience; and it may rally general public opinion (domestic or international) to the support of the nonviolent actionists. Though the effectiveness of this last factor varies greatly from one situation to another, it may produce various types of supporting actions. If repression thus produces larger numbers of nonviolent actionists, thereby increasing the defiance, and if it leads to internal dissent among the opponent's supporters, thereby reducing his capacity to deal with the defiance, it will clearly have rebounded against the opponent.

Naturally, with so many variables (including the nature of the contending groups, the issues involved, the context of the struggle, the means of repression, and the methods of nonviolent action used), in no two instances will nonviolent action "work" in exactly the same way. However, it is possible to indicate in very general terms the ways in which it does achieve results. It is, of course, sometimes defeated: no technique of action can guarantee its user short-term victory in every instance of its use. It is important to recognize, however, that failure in nonviolent action may be caused not by an inherent weakness of the technique but by weakness in the movement employing it, or in the strategy and tactics used.

Strategy is just as important in nonviolent action as it is in military action. While military strategic concepts and principles cannot be automatically carried over into the field of civilian defense, since the dynamics and mechanisms of military and nonviolent struggle differ greatly, the basic importance of strategy and tactics is in no way diminished. The attempt to cope with a variety of strategic and tactical problems associated with the application of civilian defense therefore needs to be based on thorough consideration of the particular dynamics and mechanisms of nonviolent struggle and on consideration of the general principles of strategy and tactics appropriate to the technique—both those peculiar to it and those which may be carried over from the strategy of military and other types of conflict.

THE INDIRECT APPROACH TO THE OPPONENT'S POWER

The technique of nonviolent action, and the policy of civilian defense relying upon it, can be regarded as extreme forms of the "strategy of indirect approach" which Liddell Hart has propounded in the sphere of military strategy. He has argued that a direct strategy—confronting the opponent head-on—consolidates the opponent's strength. "To move along the line of natural expectation consolidates the opponent's balance and thus increases his resisting power." An indirect approach, he argues, is militarily more sound, and generally effective results have followed when the plan of action has had "such indirectness as to ensure the opponent's unreadiness to meet it." "Dislocation" of the enemy is crucial, he insists, to achieve the conditions for victory, and the dislocation must be followed by "exploitation" of the opportunity created by the position of insecurity. It thus becomes important "to nullify opposition by paralyzing the power to oppose" and to make "the enemy do something wrong."[4]

These general, and at first glance abstract, principles of strategy can take a concrete form not only in certain types of military action but also in nonviolent action, and therefore in civilian defense. An invader, or other usurper, is likely to be best equipped to apply, and to combat, military and other violent means of combat and repression. Instead of meeting him directly on that level, nonviolent actionists and civilian defenders rely on a totally different technique of struggle, or "weapons system." The whole conflict takes on a very special character: the combatants fight, but with different weapons. Given an extensive, determined, and skillful application of nonviolent action, the opponent is likely to find that the nonviolent actionists' insistence on fighting with their chosen "weapons system" will cause him very special problems which frustrate the effective utilization of his own forces. As indicated above, the opponent's unilateral use of violent repression may only increase the resistance and win new support for the resisters, and even the opponent's supporters, agents, and soldiers may first begin to doubt the rightness of his policies and finally undertake internal opposition.

The use of nonviolent action may thus reduce or remove the very sources of the opponent's power without ever directly confronting him with the same violent means of action on which he had relied. The course of the struggle may be viewed as an attempt by the nonviolent actionists to increase their various types of strength, not only among their usual supporters but also among third parties and in the opponent's camp, and to reduce by various processes the strength of the opponent. This type of change in the relative power positions will finally determine the outcome of the struggle.

Success in nonviolent struggle depends to a very high degree on the persistence of the nonviolent actionists in fighting with *their own* methods and opposing all pressures—whether caused by emotional hostility to the opponent's brutalities, temptations of temporary gains, or *agents provocateurs* employed by the opponent (of which there have been examples)—to fight with the opponent's own, violent, methods. Violence by, or in support of, their side will sharply counter the operation of the very special mechanisms of change in nonviolent action—even when the violence is on a relatively small scale, such as rioting, injury, violent sabotage involving loss of life, or individual assassinations. The least amount of violence will, in the eyes of many, justify severe repression, and it will sharply reduce the tendency for such repression to bring sympathy and support for the nonviolent actionists, and it may well, for several reasons, reduce the number of resisters. Violence will also sharply reduce sympathy and support in the opponent's own camp.

The use of violence by, or in support of, the resisters, has many effects. Its dangers are indicated by, among other things, an examination of the likely effect on the opponent's soldiers and police, who may have become sympathetic to the resisters and reluctant to continue as opposition agents. It is well known that ordinary soldiers will fight more persistently and effectively if it is a matter of survival, and if they and their comrades are being shot, bombed, wounded, or killed. Soldiers and police acting against a nonviolent opposition and not facing such dangers may at times be inefficient in carrying out repression—for example by slackness in searches for "wanted" resisters, firing over the heads of demonstrators, or not shooting at all. In extreme cases they may openly mutiny. When such inefficiency or mutiny occurs, the opponent's power is severely threatened: this will often be an objective of nonviolent actionists or civilian defenders.

The introduction of violence by their side, however, will sharply reduce their chances of undermining opposition loyalty, as the influences producing sympathy are removed and their opponents' lives become threatened. This is simply an illustration of the point that it is very dangerous to believe that one can increase one's total combat strength by combining violent sabotage, assassinations, or types of guerrilla or conventional warfare with civilian defense, which relies on the very different technique of nonviolent action.

DEVELOPMENT OF THE TECHNIQUE

Nonviolent action has a long history, but because historians have often been more concerned with other matters much information has undoubtedly been lost. Even today, this field is largely ignored, and there is no good history of the practice and development of the technique. But it clearly began early.

A very significant pre-Gandhian expansion of the technique took place in the nineteenth and early twentieth centuries. The technique received impetus from three groups during this period: first, from trade unionists and other social radicals who sought a means of struggle—largely strikes, general strikes, and boycotts—against what they regarded as an unjust social system, and for an improvement in the condition of working men; second, from nationalists who found the technique useful in resisting a foreign enemy; and third, on the level of ideas and personal example, from individuals who wanted to show how a better society might be created.

While the use of nonviolent action by trade unionists and nationalists contributed significantly to its development, little attention was given to the refinement and improvement of the technique. Nonviolent action remained, with some exceptions, essentially passive—a counteraction to the opponent's initiatives. Religious groups like the early Quakers had practiced nonviolent action as a corporate as well as an individual reaction to persecution, but the corporate practice of this technique by nonreligious groups was almost unrelated to the idea that nonviolent behavior was morally preferable to violent behavior.

With Gandhi's experiments in the use of nonviolent action to control rulers, alter policies, and undermine political systems, the character of the technique was broadened and refinements were made in its practice. Many modifications were introduced: greater attention was given to strategy and tactics, the armory of methods was expanded, and a link was consciously forged between mass political action and the ethical principle of nonviolence. Gandhi, with his political colleagues and fellow Indians, demonstrated in a variety of conflicts in South Africa and India that nonviolent struggle could be politically effective on a large scale. He termed his refinement of the technique "satyagraha," meaning roughly insistence and reliance upon the power of truth. "In politics, its use is based upon the immutable maxim that government of the people is possible only so long as they consent either consciously or unconsciously to be governed."[5] While he sought to convert the British, he did not imagine that there could be an easy solution which would not necessitate struggle and the exercise of power. Just before the beginning of the 1930–1931 civil disobedience campaign he wrote to the Viceroy: "It is not a matter of carrying conviction by argument. The matter resolves itself into one of matching forces. Conviction or no conviction, Great Britain would defend her Indian commerce and interests by all the forces at her command. India must consequently evolve force enough to free herself from that embrace of death."[6]

Since Gandhi's time, the use of nonviolent action has spread throughout the world at an unprecedented rate. In some cases it was stimulated by Gandhi's thought and practice, but where this was so the technique was often modified in new cultural and political settings; in these cases it has already moved beyond Gandhi.

Quite independently of the campaigns led by Gandhi, important nonviolent struggles emerged under exceedingly difficult circumstances in Nazi-occupied and Communist countries: nonviolent action was used to a significant extent in the Norwegian and Danish resistance in the Second World War, in the East German uprising in 1953, in the Hungarian revolution in 1956, and in the strikes in the Soviet political prisoner camps, especially in 1953. There have been other important developments in Africa, Japan, and elsewhere. There have, of course, been setbacks, and the limited and sporadic use of nonviolent action in South Africa, for example, has been followed by advocacy of violence. However, when seen in historical perspective, there is no doubt that the technique of nonviolent action has developed very rapidly in the twentieth century.

In this same perspective, it is only recently that nonviolent resistance has been seen as a possible substitute for war in deterring or defeating invasion and other threats. It is even more recently that any attempt has been made to work out this policy —now called "civilian defense"—in any detail and that an examination of its merits and problems has been proposed.

It is inconceivable that any country will in the foreseeable future permanently abandon its defensive capacity. Threats—some genuine, some exaggerated—are too real to people; there has been too much aggression and seizure of power by dictators to be forgotten. But while defense and deterrence inevitably rely on sanctions and means of struggle, there is much reason for dissatisfaction with the usual military means. The question therefore arises whether there exists an alternative means of struggle which could be the basis of a new defense policy. Nonviolent action is an alternative means of struggle; in this, it has more in common with military struggle than with conciliation and arbitration. Could there then be a policy of civilian defense which relies on this nonviolent technique? The question must be answered, not in terms of philosophy and dogma, but in the practical examination of concrete strategies through which it might operate, the problems which might be faced, and alternative ways in which these might possibly be solved. All this will depend to a large degree on an understanding of the technique of nonviolent action, its methods, dynamics, mechanisms, and requirements.

Eighty-four Cases of Nonviolent Action

The technique of nonviolent action has been more widely practiced than is generally recognized; the following list of cases of nonviolent action should make this clear.[7] This list should also indicate—if there is still doubt—that nonviolent action is not simply an individual phenomenon, but a technique of action capable of making a powerful social and political impact. It is cases such as these which could serve as source material for research into the nature of nonviolent action and the validity of the claim that this technique can provide a functional substitute for violent conflict. The list is by no means exhaustive, nor is it either geographically or historically representative. Despite its inadequacy, it may nevertheless have an interim value as the most complete one to date.

There are many wide variations among the cases listed here: for example, in the number of participants, the degree of conscious commitment to nonviolence, the relative importance of a distinguishable leadership, the type of opponent faced, the amount of repression applied, and the objectives sought.

After each item there is an indication of the nature of the group applying the technique. In two cases the action was taken by a single individual, Gandhi, but had a major social and political effect and reduced reliance on violent conflict. These cases are indicated by IND. In six cases the action was taken by small highly committed groups, usually of less than fifty persons. These cases are indicated by SM. In the vast majority of cases, however, the action was taken by a large group, from fifty to many thousands of people. These cases are indicated by LG. These three classes were all characterized by a reliance (deliberate or accidental, principled or expedient) on nonviolent action as a part of what might be called a "grand strategy": the substitution of nonviolent action for violent conflict was almost or fully complete.

There remains, however, a small group of seven or eight cases in which the substitution of nonviolent for violent conflict was not conplete. In these cases—the Norwegian and Danish resistance during the Nazi occupation, for instance, and the Hungarian revolution—violence was not excluded on the basis of either principle or "grand strategy," and violent methods were used to a significant extent. However, in these cases nonviolent action was also used to a significant extent—up to, say, at least fifty per cent of the total "combat strength." These cases involved the use of nonviolent means of active struggle, such as strikes and noncooperation. In particular phases of these cases, nonviolent action was used almost exclusively—as for example in the resistance of the teachers and clergy in Norway, and the general strikes in Copenhagen and Amsterdam. Had such nonviolent means not been used in these cases, there might have been a relatively greater application of violent methods of conflict, or a reduction of the total "combat strength." These "mixed" cases are indicated by MX.

The eighty-four cases are classified under headings indicating the type of grievance felt by the group using nonviolent action. In several cases there is overlapping and a given case could also be listed under another heading.[8]

A. Against Oppression of Minorities

1. Civil resistance struggles by Indian minority in South Africa, 1906–14 and 1946. LG
2. Vykom temple road satyagraha (India), 1924–25. SM
3. Various campaigns in US civil rights movement, especially from 1955, such as Montgomery, Alabama, Negroes' bus boycott, 1955–56; Tallahassee, Florida, Negro bus boycott, 1956; sit-ins and freedom rides, 1961–62; the 1963 march on Washington, DC; and other cases. LG
4. Civil resistance by Tamils in Ceylon, 1956–57, etc., and 1961. LG

B. Against Exploitation and Other Economic Grievances

1. Mysore (India) noncooperation, 1830. LG
2. Irish rent strike and tax refusal, 1879–86. MX
3. Boycott of Captain Boycott by Irish peasants, 1880. LG
4. Buck's Stove and Range boycott (US), 1907. LG
5. British general strike, 1926. LG
6. US sit-down strikes, 1936–37. LG
7. French sit-down strikes, 1936–37. LG
8. "Reverse strikes," various cases in Italy, at least since 1950, including mass fast and reverse strike in Sicily led by Danilo Dolci, 1956. LG
9. General strike in Gambia, January 1961. LG
10. Spanish workers' strikes in the Asturias mines and elsewhere, 1962. LG

(Many other cases of strikes and boycotts could be included here, and would greatly add to the number of cases of use in the technique in the West.)

C. Against Communal Disorders

1. Gandhi's fast in Calcutta, 1947. IND
2. Gandhi's fast in Delhi, 1948. IND

D. On Religious Issues

1. Early Christians' reaction to Roman persecution. LG
2. Early Quakers' resistance to persecution in England, late seventeenth century. LG
3. Roman Catholic struggle vs. Prussian Government over mixed marriages, 1836–40. LG
4. Roman Catholic resistance vs. Bismarck in *Kulturkampf* (conflict of civilizations), 1871–87 (though concessions began in 1878). LG
5. *Khilafat* (Caliphate) satyagraha (India), 1920–22. LG
6. Akali Sikhs' reform satyagraha (India), 1922. LG
7. South Vietnam Buddhist campaign vs. Ngo regime, 1963. LG.

E. Against Particular Injustices and Administrative Excesses

1. Economic boycotts and tax refusal in American colonies, 1763–76. LG
2. Quebec farmers' and villagers' noncooperation with the British *corvée* system, 1776–78. LG
3. Persian anti-tobacco-tax boycott, 1891. LG
4. German Social Democrats' struggle vs. Bismarck, 1879–90. LG
5. Belgian general strikes for broader suffrage, 1893, 1902, and 1913. LG
6. Swedish three-day general strike for extension of suffrage, 1902. LG
7. English tax-refusal vs. tax aid for private schools, 1902–14. LG
8. Chinese anti-Japanese boycotts in 1906, 1908, 1915 and 1919. LG
9. "Free speech" campaign by Industrial Workers of the World in Sioux City, Iowa, 1914–15. LG
10. Kheda (India) peasants' resistance, 1918. LG
11. Peasants' passive resistance in USSR, post-1918. LG
12. Rowlatt Act satyagraha (India), 1919. LG
13. Bardoli (India) peasants' revenue refusal, 1928. LG
14. Pardi (India) satyagraha, 1950. LG
15. Manbhum, Bihar (India), resistance movement, 1950. LG
16. Nonviolent seizure of Heligoland from RAF, 1951. SM
17. South Indian Telugu agitation for new state of Andra, pre-1953. LG
18. Political prisoners' strike at Vorkuta, USSR, 1953. LG
19. Finnish general strike, 1956. LG
20. African bus boycotts in Johannesburg, Pretoria, Port Elizabeth and Bloemfontein, 1957. LG
21. Kerala (India) nonviolent resistance vs. elected Communist government's education policy, etc., 1959. LG

22. Argentine general strike, 1959. LG
23. Belgian general strike, 1960–61. LG

F. *Against War and War Preparations*

1. New Zealand anticonscription struggles, 1912–14 and 1930. LG
2. Argentine general strike vs. possible entry into World War I, 1917. LG
3. French, English, and Irish dock workers' strike against military intervention in Russia, 1920. LG
4. League of Nations' economic sanctions vs. Italy during war on Abyssinia, 1935–36. LG
5. Japanese resistance to constructing a US air base at Sunakawa, 1956. LG
6. Voyages of the *Golden Rule* and *Phoenix,* 1958, and of *Everyman I* and *Everyman II,* 1962, in efforts to stop US nuclear tests in the Pacific; and of *Everyman III* against Soviet nuclear tests, 1962. SM
7. Various cases of civil disobedience and other nonviolent action in Britain in support of nuclear disarmament, organized by the Direct Action Committee Against Nuclear War and the Committee of 100, 1958–63. SM and LG
8. Attempted "invasion" to prevent atomic test at Reggane, French North African atomic testing site, 1959–60. SM
9. Various cases of civil disobedience and other nonviolent action in the US, largely organized by the Committee for Nonviolent Action, 1959–66. SM and LG
10. Demonstration, threat of general strike, and various acts of intervention, to forestall new civil war in Algeria, August-September 1962. LG

G. *Against Long-established Undemocratic Rule*

1. Roman plebeians vs. patricians, 494 BC. LG
2. Major aspects of Netherlands' resistance vs. Spanish rule, especially 1565–76. MX
3. Hungarian passive resistance vs. Austria, 1850–67. LG
4. Finnish resistance to Russian rule, 1898–1905. LG
5. Major aspects of 1905 revolution in imperial Russia, including general strikes, parallel government, and various types of noncooperation. MX
6. Korean national protest vs. Japanese rule, 1919–22. LG
7. Egyptian passive resistance vs. British rule, 1919–22. LG
8. Western Samoan resistance vs. New Zealand rule, 1919–36. LG

9. Indian independence struggle, especially campaigns of 1930–31, 1932–34, 1940–41 and 1942. LG
10. General strike in El Salvador vs. Martinez dictatorship, 1944. LG
11. General strike in Guatemala vs. Ubico regime, 1944. LG
12. South African defiance campaign, 1952. LG
13. East German uprising, June 1953. LG (MX?)
14. Nonviolent "invasion" of Goa, 1955. LG
15. General strike and economic shut-down vs. Haitian strongman General Magliore, 1956. LG
16. Major aspects of the Hungarian revolution, 1956–57. MX
17. Barcelona and Madrid bus boycotts, 1957. LG
18. Nonviolent resistance to British rule in Nyasaland, 1957. LG
19. South African Pan-Africanists' defiance of pass laws, 1960. LG
20. International boycotts and embargoes on South African products, from 1960. LG

H. Against New Attempts to Impose Undemocratic Rule

1. Kanara (India) non-cooperation, 1799–1800. LG
2. German workers' general strike vs. the Kapp *putsch,* March 1920. LG
3. Ruhr passive resistance vs. French and Belgian occupation, 1923. LG
4. Major aspects of the Dutch resistance, 1940–45, including several important strikes. MX
5. Major aspects of the Danish resistance, 1940–45, including the Copenhagen general strike, 1944. MX
6. Major aspects of the Norwegian resistance, 1940–45. MX
7. General strike in Haiti vs. Provisional President Pierre-Louis, 1957. LG
8. British and UN economic sanctions vs. Rhodesia, from 1965. LG

(Many of these actions were in support of the legitimate regime.)

The very considerable differences among these struggles, in the types of issues, the groups involved, the countries, cultural and historical backgrounds, etc., should be noted. Although the list is neither complete nor representative, a few very tentative conclusions can be drawn which suggest that some widely held views about the technique of nonviolent action may be inaccurate.

Forty-eight of these cases took place in the "West" (including Russia); twenty-three in the "East"; nine in Africa; and one in Australasia. Three were international. Something less than forty percent took place in "democracies" (roughly defined), and slightly more than sixty percent under "dictatorships" (including foreign occupations and seven cases under totalitarian systems). In some of these cases the nonviolent actionists partly or fully succeeded in achieving the desired objectives, and in other cases —for example, many of the antiwar actions—they failed. In not more than nine of these eighty-four cases were both the leadership and the participants pacifist.

Even making allowances for an incomplete and unrepresentative list, these figures are sufficient to challenge the conception that nonviolent action is mainly an "Eastern" phenomenon, that it is only applied under "democratic" conditions, that it is suitable only for convinced pacifists, and that it ignores the existence of conflicts and power.

LEARNING FROM THE PAST

Generally speaking, very little effort has been made to learn from past cases of nonviolent action with a view to increasing our understanding of the nature of the technique, and gaining knowledge which might be useful in future struggles, or which might contribute to an expansion of the use of nonviolent action instead of violence. Study of past cases[9] could provide the basis for a more informed assessment of the future political potentialities of the technique.

There are far too few detailed documentary accounts of past uses of nonviolent action; such accounts can provide raw material for analyses of particular facets of the technique and help in the formulation of hypotheses which might be tested in other situations. An important step, therefore, in the development of research in this field is the preparation of purely factual accounts of a large number of specific cases of nonviolent action, accompanied if possible with collections of existing interpretations and explanations of the events.

A compilation, more extensive than the preliminary listing above, of as many instances of socially or politically significant nonviolent action as can be discovered is also needed, and should preferably include a few standard major facts about the cases, and bibliographic clues. Such a survey could help in the selection of the cases meriting more detailed investigation; and it would make possible more authoritative comparisons of the cases with particular factors in mind, such as the geographical, historical, and cultural distribution of the cases, the types of issues involved, and the types of opponents against whom nonviolent struggles have been waged.

Another subject which deserves careful study is the meaning of, and conditions for, success in nonviolent action. The varying meanings of the terms "success" and "defeat" need to be distinguished, and consideration given to concrete achievements in particular struggles. The matter is much more complex than may at first appear. For example, failure within a short period of time to get an invader to withdraw fully from an occupied country may nevertheless be accompanied by the frustration of several of the invader's objectives, the maintenance of a considerable degree of autonomy within the "conquered" country, and the furtherance of a variety of changes in the invader's own regime and homeland; these changes may themselves later lead either to the desired full withdrawal, or to further relaxation of occupation rule. When various types of "success" and "defeat" have been distinguished, it would be desirable to have a study of the conditions under which they have occurred in the past and seem possible in the future. These conditions would include factors in the social and political situation, the nature of the issues in the conflict, the type of opponent and his repression, the type of group using nonviolent action, the type of nonviolent action used (taking into account quality, extent, strategy, tactics, methods, persistence in face of repression, etc.), and lastly the possible role and influence of "third parties."

The question of the viability and political practicality of the technique of nonviolent action is one which can be investigated by research and analysis, and it is possible that the efficiency and political potentialities of this technique can be increased by deliberate efforts. The question of violent or nonviolent means in politics and defense, if tackled in this manner, is removed from the sphere of "belief" or "nonbelief" and opened up for investigation and research.

NOTES

1. For a fuller discussion of this approach to political power see Gene Sharp," 'The Political Equivalent of War'—Civilian Defense," *International Conciliation,* no. 555 (November 1965), 20–29.
2. For a definition of "pacifism," see Gene Sharp, Appendix Two of *Civilian Defense,* Adam Roberts et al. (London: Peace News, 1964).
3. See Gene Sharp, "The Politics of Nonviolent Action," unpublished manuscript, Center for International Affairs (Harvard University, Cambridge, Mass., 1966), vol. 1, chaps. 8–13.
4. B. H. Liddell Hart, *Strategy: The Indirect Approach* (London: Faber and Faber, 1954), pp. 25, 349, 359, and 350. Also published under the title *Strategy* (New York: Praeger, 1954).
5. M. K. Gandhi, *Indian Opinion,* Golden Number, 1914. Quoted in Gandhi, *Satyagraha* (Ahmedabad: Navajivan, 1951), p. 35. Also published under the title *Nonviolent Resistance* (New York: Schocken Books, 1961).
6. All-India Congress Committee, *Congress Bulletin,* 7 (March 1930), no. 5. Quoted in Sharp, *Gandhi Wields the Weapon of Moral Power* (Ahmedabad: Navajivan, 1960), p. 64. For a brief discussion of some popular misconceptions about Gandhi and his activities, see Gene Sharp, "Gandhi's Political Significance Today," in *Gandhi: His Relevance for Our Times,* ed. G. Ramachandran and T. K. Mahadevan (Bombay: Bharatiya Vidya Bhavan, 1964), pp. 44–66; 2d ed., 1967, pp. 137–157.
7. This section listing cases of nonviolent action is a substantially revised version of Sharp, Appendix One, in Roberts *et al., Civilian Defence* (London: Peace News, 1964), pp. 58–62.
8. This list has been compiled from a wide variety of sources, including newspaper reports, magazine articles, pamphlets, personal knowledge, and especially Clarence Marsh Case, *Non-violent Coercion: A Study in Methods of Social Pressure* (New York and London: Century Co., 1923); Barthelemy de Ligt, *The Conquest of Violence: An Essay on War and Revolution* (London: Routledge, 1937); Ranganath R. Diwakar, *Satyagraha: Its Technique and History* (Bombay: Hind Kitabs, 1946; and E. T. Hiller, *The Strike: A Study in Collective Action* (Chicago: University of Chicago Press, 1928). A pioneering list of nine cases of nonviolent action in Canada, prepared by Dan Daniels, was published in *Our Generation Against Nuclear War,* 3:1 (Montreal, June 1964).
9. A preliminary, but nevertheless valuable, listing of literature on the subject is April Carter, David Hoggett, and Adam Roberts, *Nonviolent Action: Theory and Practice—A Selected Bibliography,* Housmans, London, 1966.

12 Some Questions on Civilian Defense

THOMAS C. SCHELLING

One has to admit that it could work. "Structures of power (governments, social organizations) always depend upon the voluntary cooperation of great numbers of individuals even when the structures seem to rely on physical force. The chief wielders of power, in other words, must have the assistance and cooperation of hundreds or even thousands of persons for the administration of physical force. The task of those who oppose a structure having physical force at its command is, therefore, to persuade hundreds of men to refuse any longer to cooperate with the tyrant or other administrator of violence . . ." (Mulford Q. Sibley, ed., *The Quiet Battle* [New York: Doubleday, 1963], p. 9).

From *Civilian Resistance as a National Defense: Non-Violent Action against Aggression,* Adam Roberts, ed. (Harrisburg, Pa.: Stackpole Books, 1968), pp. 302–308. This book was also published in England under the title *The Strategy of Civilian Defence* (London: Faber and Faber Ltd., 1967). Reprinted (slightly abridged) by permission of the editor and publishers.

This is the starting point, whether our concern is resisting the tyrant or promoting his regime, frustrating a military victor or helping to establish his control. The fruits of conquest—nearly all of them, though not quite all—depend on *affirmative* action by large numbers of people. Force cannot procure it directly. You can drag a horse to water, but only he can make his muscles work; and if he won't drink, you'll shortly have no horse.

It is the *threat* of pain, privation, and loss that may induce people to cooperate. Inflicting the plan and damage gives the tyrant, or the military victor, nothing directly. If people can be made immune to threats—because they cannot comprehend what is wanted of them, because they cannot comprehend what will be done to them, or because they are motivated to refuse compliance even in the face of threats—violence will get you nowhere unless you want merely to exterminate or to immobilize or to impoverish the population, to expel it from its territory, to carry away its physical assets, or to make an example that will appeal to some other people in some other territory.

Fiction may prove the point better than historical documentation. We can imagine a militarily defenseless people thoroughly confounding a conqueror by sitting quietly, perhaps not eating, threatening to deprive him of any subjects by dying on his hands. He may let them die; he may even kill them; but exploit them he cannot. And if his subjects truly believe that life on this earth is but a chance to earn access to paradise after death, if they believe that nonviolent noncooperation earns entrance, and especially if suicide is permitted to avoid involuntary collaboration under the stimulus of pain or hunger, the people may quietly die, to the embarrassment and frustration of their conqueror.

If he anticipates it, perhaps he will not even conquer them. He can still take their belongings, eliminate them as a military threat, deny their territory to some other opponent, or achieve whatever else comes from the extinction of these people who will not become his subjects; but if he wants to rule a viable economy populated by human beings this can be denied him.

At least, in fiction it can, and in science fiction chemical or electronic substitutes might be found for the beliefs and values that would otherwise do the trick. Whether actual human beings, the residents of an actual contemporary country, can take advantage of this principle in frustrating a tyrant (or, better still, in deterring his conquest before it occurs) is the question to which this book [*Civilian Resistance as a National Defense,* see note p. 172] is addressed. And the answer, as I discern it in the chapters of this book, is that we do not know. The principle is undeniable, but we have not yet been given evidence that live human beings in today's world can so embody the principle in their organized behavior as to make the tyrant quit the effort, to disarm him of his bureaucrats and soldiers, or to dissuade him to advance.

Of course, the principle may work unintentionally. If nobody seems terribly eager to recolonize the former Belgian Congo, it may be because some societies appear incapable of responding to authority or of submitting even to a benevolent effort at discipline. Impotence may be as impressive as the threat of disciplined nonviolent resistance in dissuading conquerors. The world is full of animals that enjoy freedom because nobody knows how to domesticate them. As Russell Baker has pointed out, the dolphins should take a lesson from the cats, not from the dogs and the monkeys; dogs have come to heel and monkeys to work for hurdy-gurdy men because people know that dogs and monkeys can understand what is demanded of them and what the consequences of rebellion are, while the cats have got a reputation for indiscipline and poor learning, and are accorded privacy and freedom. If the dolphins, in their conceit, show that they can hear what is said to them and can evaluate consequences, they will become prime candidates for slavery.

Disciplined nonviolence—an overriding unwillingness to comply—has this unique defensive quality: if you successfully communicate it, it makes you totally immune to threats. If it is known that no sanctions, no penalties, no inducements can make one behave, then *purposive* threats are of no avail. One may still be punished for spite or revenge, or in disbelief that noncompliance can persist, but when the tyrant is convinced that no sanctions will work, that he can no more successfully command his defenseless populace than he can command vegetables, his authority is gone, he knows it, and even punishment becomes a chore, not a source of authority. Xerxes whipped the waters of the Hellespont for their turbulence when he wanted to cross his army over; an objective of nonviolent resistance—indeed, of completely inactive submissiveness—would be to persuade the dictator that punishment and blandishments would be of no more avail than whipping the waters or pouring jars of honey into them.

Technically, though, the tyrant and his subjects are in somewhat symmetrical positions. *They* can deny *him* most of what *he* wants—they can, that is, if they have the disciplined organization to refuse collaboration. And *he* can deny *them* just about everything *they* want—he can deny it by using the force at his command. They can deny him the economic fruits of conquest, he can deny them the economic fruits of their own activity. They can deny him the satisfaction of ruling a disciplined country, he can deny them the satisfaction of ruling themselves. They can confront him with chaos, starvation, idleness, and social breakdown, but he confronts them with the same thing and, indeed, most of what they deny him they deny themselves. It is a bargaining situation in which either side, if adequately disciplined and organized, can deny most of what the other wants; and it remains to be seen who wins. My immediate point is not that the tyrant is bound to win, merely that the best organized and best disciplined resistance, if it takes the form of refusal to collaborate, only converts what would have been an asymmetry of force into a two-sided bargaining situation, with no guarantee that the "resisters" will win.

And note that *win* is what they have to do if "civilian defense" is to work. Compromise is not enough. This book is not about nonviolence and organized civilian resistance as a method of protest, as a method of alleviating conditions, as a method of denying a conqueror *some* of what he wants and of coming to terms with him. This book is not about how to improve the terms of surrender, how to live better under military occupation, or how to make a tyrannical regime become gradually more civilized. It is a book about defense and deterrence, and the proposition is that disciplined, organized civilian nonviolent resistance can actually make the conqueror withdraw (or at least make his military occupation utterly nominal) or dissuade him from conquest in advance.

The proposition is not merely that the Danes—had Hitler won his war and covered Europe with his Nazi regime—might have ameliorated that regime by skillful use of nonviolent resistance. The proposition is not merely that the Dutch could sabotage Hitler's military effort by some acts of nonviolent opposition. The proposition has to be that a regime could actually be overthrown, or made to retire, or dissuaded from conquest in the first place, by the use or the prospect of nonviolent resistance. Otherwise we are dealing not with "defense" but with protest, with political action, with a bargaining technique that leads to compromise and accommodation.

The proposition is easy to establish in its weaker form. If one merely proposes that nonviolence can be an effective bargaining technique, whether used by striking workers, by an oppressed minority, or by the bulk of a population against a nonrepresentative government, or if it is proposed that a good way to deal with a military conqueror, after one has been defeated militarily, is to revert to disciplined nonviolence, the case is a strong one. If it were proposed that a conqueror could be weakened in his conduct of war elsewhere by some organized nonviolent sabotage, so that his eventual military defeat would come more quickly, a good case would be made for some countries at some times.

And perhaps if one is willing to allow unlimited time to seduce a conqueror or his local representatives, to impress him and to teach him, even to negotiate eventual decolonization, the case for nonviolence is surely substantiated by history, though perhaps often with the threat of violence lurking in the background. (Considering the abortive result of so many revolutions that supplant one tyranny with another, one can wish that more rebellious cliques and revolutionary movements around the world had the patience and the discipline to rely on "civilian defense," not only because it might minimize violence but because it might improve the quality of the regimes that succeed those that are overthrown.)

But the proposition is a stronger one. It is that a country—in particular, a country that has a real alternative of military defense, and by implication a country of western Europe or North America—can successfully substitute "civilian defense" altogether for its military effort to deter or to defend itself. And this must be a hard case to make; otherwise this book would have made it.

A critical question is whether nonviolent methods are compatible with the threat or the actual use of violence. The answer seems to depend on at least three circumstances. First, are the morale, discipline, and leadership that nonviolence requires compatible with the exercise of violence? Second, in dealing with the adversary, does the occurrence of violence undermine much of what nonviolence is trying to achieve by providing an excuse for revenge, by abandoning the claim to moral superiority, and by exacerbating relations between the subject people and the bureaucracy of the tyrant? Third, can the violence be handled by some third party, as in the case of the Allies against Hitler, while other dissidents harass the regime "nonviolently"?

The case for pure nonviolence is stronger if the object is protest rather than defense. If one is trying to reach accommodation with a tyrant, resort to violence may spoil a nonviolent bargaining campaign, but if one is actually trying to make a tyrant retreat or withdraw, it is not clear that nonviolence by itself is up to the job, at least within the time span that the word "defense" suggests.

A more intriguing question is raised by the term "defense." In the West we have got used (and perhaps in the East as well) to a good many euphemisms for words like "war," "military," and others that are neutral or symmetrical in their moral implications. What about civilian *offense?* Are the techniques of "civilian defense" equally available to an aggressor, who needs only to support a disciplined dissident group to cause the downfall of a regime? Was not the original conception of Communist conquest one of "civilian offense"? Are not the techniques of "civilian defense" against a tyrant or against any regime that one wishes to overthrow just as pertinent to revolution as to defense, and as susceptible to aggressively and externally inspired revolution as to purely indigenous revolt?

Let me raise an even more serious question. Is there any reason to suppose that the techniques of nonviolent resistance are more available to good people than to bad, to right causes than to wrong, to democrats than to demagogues, or to defense than to offense? There is of course reason to suppose that these techniques are *comparatively* more available to the dispossessed than to the wealthy, to the weak than to the strong; those who have a capacity for violence have an alternative; those who have not, lack the alternative. Nonviolence has a *comparative* advantage for the defeated that it does not have for the victor, because the victor has the alternative of force. Nonviolence thus sometimes has a comparative advantage for the poor, the weak, the disfranchised, because they lack the trappings of power and force. (They do not necessarily lack the capacity for violence against people and property, so nonviolence has to compete with terrorism; I wish it competed better.) There may also be an argument that nonviolence demands moral qualities that are usually absent in the more vicious regimes, like those that have worn black shirts or boots and belts and masks.

Still, terror may be most effective when disciplined, and if the discipline is present, nonviolence may be an alternative. Passive resistance has been notoriously the technique by which nonintegrating Southern states have frustrated the federal government in America. Civil rights in America is a good case to keep in mind, because it lacks the bilateral simplicity of so many adversary relations. There are two minorities, a Negro minority and a white minority; both have used nonviolence and passive resistance, one of them against the military forces of the United States.

The movement of M. Poujade in France suggests that nonviolence is as pertinent, say, to the rich who prefer not to pay income taxes as to the poor who prefer not to be taxed for the conduct of foreign wars, as pertinent to the well-to-do farmer as to the poor one who wants better credit, better legal aid, more land, or more education for his children.

Mulford Sibley's words can be inspirational or frightening, according to *whose* noncooperation you have in mind and what kind of regime the nonviolent resisters wish to impose. "Structures of power" and "wielders of power" may indeed sound like tyrants, oligarchies, and military occupation forces, but they may also include the United Nations, the Supreme Court of the United States, or a regime trying desperately to become democratic in a country with a military or authoritarian tradition.

The most disturbing question raised by all these discussions of nonviolence is, which target is more vulnerable? Is it a militarily rampant Hitler, or the Weimar Republic? Is it the segregated South or the Supreme Court of the United States? Is it France under the Fifth Republic or France under the Fourth? Is it the University of Peking or the University of California?

It would be nice if all good things clustered together, and nonviolence (which sounds so much better than violence) had a necessary affinity for the good and the right and the pure—for the meek and all those who should inherit the earth. Maybe it does, but we do not know it yet. The potential of nonviolence is enormous. Mulford Sibley has quietly pointed out that it knows almost no limits. In the end it could be as important as nuclear fission. Like nuclear fission it has implications for peace, war, stability, terror, confidence, and international and domestic politics, that are not easy yet to assess.

V   Epilogue

13 Contrasting Approaches to Conflict

MARGARET W. FISHER

Throughout recorded history, human responses to conflict have ranged widely from a zestful enjoyment of conflict situations as a test of personal strength and courage all the way to an anguished yearning to be free from the necessity for engaging in conflict. Culturally approved responses have at different times established modes for the conduct of conflict which molded whole societies. The significance of the selection of such a mode from the various possible approaches to conflict can be demonstrated by examining two which differ radically in their basic premises. These are the Gandhian approach through which satyagraha was evolved and a mode derived from a relatively new "science of efficient action" known as praxeology.

Gandhian satyagraha ("adherence to truth") asserts the relevance of moral values, defines ends in terms of engaging the adversary in a search for "truth," insists upon nonviolent means, and stresses the bonds of common humanity linking the opposing sides. A basic human capacity to both display and respond affirmatively to moral courage is assumed. Stemming from this assumption is the conviction that voluntary and unflinching acceptance of suffering—to the death, if need be—will ultimately arouse compassion in the most stony-hearted adversary, making reconciliation possible.

The praxeological approach, on the other hand, elevates efficiency above all other values, takes no account of any ethical, moral, or emotional aspects of conflict except insofar as they may affect efficiency, seeks either victory or the denial of victory to the opponent, restricts means only by criteria based upon expediency, and assumes a basic need to guard at all times against human depravity. So important is that branch of praxeological theory dealing with conflict that a special term, agonology ("science of struggle"), has been proposed for it. That suggestion has been adopted here.

For the refinement of concepts as well as for the coinage of the terms satyagraha (from Sanskrit roots) and agonology (from Greek roots), we are heavily indebted to the seminal efforts of two men: Mohandas K. Gandhi (1869–1948), a deeply religious social reformer and political activist whose original profession was the law;[1] and Tadeusz Kotarbiński (1886–), a philosopher and logician whose academic career reflects a major interest in a scientific approach to the theory of knowledge.[2] Among the voluminous supplements to Gandhi's writings, an outstanding contribution has been made by Joan Bondurant.[3] Useful in conjunction with Kotarbiński's writings[4] is Norman Bailey's brief survey of the status of conflict theory, in the course of which he introduced the Polish philosopher to American social scientists.[5]

Kotarbiński's treatise on praxeology had its beginnings in an effort to raise the level of efficiency of Poland's factories. Broadening the scope of his inquiry in the hope of constructing a general theory of efficient action, Kotarbiński scanned a wide range of published materials (although he did not refer either to the Gandhian experience or to the Indian classic, the *Arthashastra,* which has reportedly been translated into Russian several times). Beginning with Polish folklore, (which he found "unfortunate in its maxims justifying negligence, slovenliness, and laziness"), he went on to consult the works of moralists, writers of fables, literary figures, scientists, and thinkers from various fields from the Greek philosophers down to modern studies of business administration, game theory, and the like, with particular attention to the theory of events and the theory of complex wholes.

In all his reading Kotarbiński came upon no strictly praxeological literature, although he did find praxeological "motifs" of importance in sources as diverse as Aristotle, La Fontaine, Defoe's *Robinson Crusoe,* Karl Marx, and Talcott Parsons, to name but a few of the writers to whom he has accorded special mention. The one work he found that dealt with a general theory of conflict was a small book on chess by Dr. Emanuel Lasker, the German mathematician who once held the world chess championship for nearly three decades.[6]

From these researches Kotarbiński emerged with several sobering reflections. He concluded that all observations concerning the effectiveness of purposive action had already been made, leaving to the theorist only systematization and quantitative precision. He was "embarrassed" that no distinct discipline had yet developed for formulating a grammar of action.[7] He confessed that he himself was not entirely free from doubt that general praxeological theory "had no content over and above vague generalities," and conceded that there might be some truth in the criticism that "the more general a given praxeological maxim the more trivial the idea it contains."[8] He appeared ready to accept praxeology as a codifier of truisms concerning practical behavior and to be satisfied if his own work contributed to the "registering and ordering of existing concepts."[9]

The two contrasting modes for dealing with conflict, agonology and satyagraha, evolved in entirely different ways. Kotarbiński's treatise on praxeology was based largely on the examination and analysis by a senior scholar—he was nearly seventy when it was published—of the practical wisdom of mankind available to him in libraries. Interestingly enough, one of the points upon which he laid emphasis was the importance of the "compulsory situation" as a prerequisite to progress. In a very real sense, satyagraha can be looked upon as the outgrowth of a "compulsory situation" in which Gandhi, as a young man in his early twenties, found himself. In the event, he proved a striking example of its creative potential.

The details of this compulsory situation are readily to be found in Gandhi's own autobiographical writings. For our present purposes, a few points are all that need to be made. First, the young Gandhi, as a London-trained barrister, arrived in South Africa totally unprepared for the racism that subjected him to crude attacks upon his self-esteem and violent assaults upon his person. His first impulse was to leave the country immediately, but he found the courage to reject this emotional response and to stay on.

The year he so unwillingly remained in South Africa proved to be a major turning point in his career. His activities, demonstrably very different from what they would have been had he stayed in India, set the pattern for much that was to follow. During this year Gandhi came to realize that his talents as a lawyer lay in his ability to persuade adversaries to compose their differences out of court rather than in the usual adversary proceedings.

This was also the year that Gandhi, who by his own account had never before engaged in reading anything not connected with his schoolwork or professional training, had the leisure to indulge in reading. Again unlike Kotarbiński, who had consulted the world's practical wisdom, Gandhi sought to find his way out of his difficulties in otherworldly wisdom. He studied and discussed with friends the scriptures of all the world's great faiths. He concluded that all religions contained at least a core of truth, and accepted Christ, Daniel, and Socrates as models to be emulated. All three had voluntarily accepted an agonizing death and in so doing had powerfully affected men's minds and hearts down through the ages.

Important as these ideas were to the development of satyagraha, the most significant outcome of this unusual year may well have been the capacity he achieved for mastering anger. As he once put it: "I have learnt through bitter experience the one supreme lesson to conserve my anger and as heat conserved is transmuted into energy, even so our anger controlled can be transmuted into a power which can move the world."[10] The immediate result of this capacity was an increase in his personal effectiveness, enabling him to become a leader of men much older than himself. In later years it also served to bind to him disciples whom he particularly prized: young terrorists who, learning from him how to control anger, forsook violence for the more challenging effort of practicing the "nonviolence of the strong."

The end of Gandhi's obligatory year did not, however, terminate his stay in South Africa. He first postponed his return to India for one month to lead a fight against proposed legislation threatening Indian rights. Then the month lengthened into years as the local government, alarmed by the rapid growth of the Indian population, adopted new restrictive devices as earlier ones were weakened or eliminated. Throughout his efforts for Indians in South Africa, Gandhi was consciously preparing himself for greater labors in India. He undertook experiments of various kinds, within a "model" community which he established, aimed at developing maximum village self-sufficiency with respect to food, shelter, clothing, health, and education. When Gandhi, at 45, finally returned to his homeland, his achievements had already established his reputation. He was himself full of confidence in his plans for social and political reform and in satyagraha as a "sovereign remedy" for all of India's ills.

What was the nature of this remedy? The word satyagraha has been Anglicized and has gained wide acceptance, but the tendency has been to narrow its meaning to nonviolent mass civil disobedience. Such campaigns were indeed the most dramatic of Gandhi's many experiments, but from the beginning the term encompassed other modes of protest, including both group and individual action in the form of such efforts as strikes, fasts, and demonstrations, whether or not laws were disobeyed in the process.

Gandhi's initial attempts to apply his remedy in India were remarkably successful. Twice his mere readiness to undertake such campaigns was enough by itself to bring about the capitulation of local authorities. Gandhi began to visualize not only the transformation of India, but through India, of the world. In this mood, he requested a friend to draw up a list, for every state in India, of cases of hardship arising either from laws or from the manner of their enforcement. Local leaders everywhere received encouragement from him to make their own experiments with satyagraha.

With more experience, however, his euphoria waned. Not all campaigns that were called satyagraha seemed to him worthy of the name. The high potential that he saw in it made him all the more anxious to preserve its character of "righteous struggle," in which, he wrote, "there are no secrets to be guarded, no scope for cunning, and no place for untruth."[11] He was particularly concerned by the ever-present danger of the eruption of violence. When, after some years of trial and error, Gandhi came at last to feel that he had "mastered the technique of satyagraha," he made it clear that for him it was a complete way of life, and no "mere technique of struggle." The civil disobedience campaigns, he said, were the "aggressive aspects" of satyagraha. Its "profound" and "permanent aspect" consisted in peaceful experimentation with constructive programs with which he hoped to bring about Hindu-Muslim unity and promote economic and social justice for India's most downtrodden.[12]

For Gandhi, then, a prior concern with conflict as a means for effecting change gave way for a time to preoccupation with conciliation and integration. This shift in emphasis made it all the more necessary that satyagraha should live up to its highest ethical potential and not be resorted to lightly. Indeed, a trend—not fully consistent—toward narrowing the use of civil disobedience became discernible. The initial encouragement to wide experimentation with satyagraha gave way to restrictions on who should lead such campaigns and then to reductions in the number of participants, until at one point Gandhi himself became for a time the sole satyagrahi.

There are difficulties in any attempt to make a concise statement on the essential ingredients of satyagraha as Gandhi saw them, in part because the record of his doings and sayings is overwhelmingly voluminous and in part because of the many contradictions that record contains. Gandhi, engaged as he was in a lifelong search for truth as disclosed through action, always considered words to be less important than action, whether the words in question were his own or another's. Consistency he valued perhaps even less than did Emerson, whom he delighted to quote. When followers, perturbed by contradictory positions he had taken, brought their dilemmas to him for resolution, Gandhi, more amused than otherwise, would advise them to heed only his latest statement. Indeed, in the last months of his life he went so far as to recommend that all his writings be burned, since he considered his life to be his message.

Fortunately, this drastic counsel was not followed, but it does leave us in a somewhat difficult position. These difficulties are not made any easier by Gandhi's characteristic refusal to accede to requests either to draw up general principles for satyagraha or to write a treatise on nonviolence. Action, not "academic writings," was his domain, Gandhi said. "What I understand, according to my lights, to be my duty, and what comes my way, I do." And again, "I can give no guarantee that I will do or believe tomorrow, what I do or hold to be true today."[13] With respect to satyagraha, however, Joan Bondurant has surmounted the difficulty boldly, abstracting general principles from an examination of selected campaigns. Her formulations have left all students of satyagraha in her debt, and the statements concerning satyagraha in the chart that follows rely heavily upon her work.[14] The statements concerning agonology I have abstracted from Kotarbiński's discussion.[15] Of course, no chart could do justice to the richness of the original discussions, both of which should be consulted.

OBJECTIVES AND DIRECTIVES: GANDHIAN SATYAGRAHA
AND AGONOLOGY

Satyagraha	Agonology

Objective

To achieve an agreement with the opponent acceptable to both sides, by engaging him in a search for "truth," using only nonviolent means.	To defeat the opponent, or at least to avoid being defeated, using whatever means may be expedient.

Directives

Search for avenues of cooperation with the opponent on honorable terms; never take advantage of his difficulties.	Make the opponent's position as difficult as possible; make difficulties for both sides if they will embarrass the opponent more than they will you.
Protect the opponent's person and his resources.	Strike first at the opponent's most vital parts; use his resources against him.
Reduce your demands to a minimum consistent with truth.	Try to leave your opponent only one way out.
Avoid a static condition, but launch direct action only after exhausting all other efforts to achieve an honorable settlement.	Economize your resources, but ensure your own freedom of movement and restrict the opponent's even at some loss to yourself.
Never lie; hold nothing back; keep the opponent, the public, and participants informed as an integral part of the movement.	Deceive the opponent. In general, refuse to disclose your intentions, but disclose them occasionally; the opponent may be deceived, or his next move be made more predictable by you.
Extend areas of rationality.	Commit "irrational" acts at times to confuse the opponent.

The entries in this chart are illustrative rather than exhaustive and are not fully comparable in all respects. It could scarcely be otherwise. Satyagraha, which began as a means for securing the redress of grievances suffered by a disadvantaged group at the hands of the dominant elements in South African society, evolved into a complex technique of action which had the potential, for those who chose to practice it, of changing the quality of their lives through its emphasis on ethics in action. Agonology, on the other hand, was not only codified from centuries of largely unhappy human experience but was also generalized to cover a broad spectrum of situations: from games with only two contestants through sports involving teamwork all the way to warfare between coalitions of nation states.

Agonology employs a strategy of deceit, lays emphasis on economy insofar as it is a component of efficiency, but relies even more heavily on keeping options open if the two principles are in conflict. Satyagraha employs a "truth" strategy stressing honor and rejects out of hand all options inconsistent with truth and honor. And although it sometimes came about that what Gandhi's sense of honor demanded on a given occasion could change with changing circumstances, it must also be said that satyagraha in his hands represented an ideal so lofty that few, if any, actual campaigns were felt by him to have maintained their purity unsullied. The precepts of agonology, on the other hand, are familiar enough as wartime expedients made palatable, temporarily at least, by the fervor of an enhanced love of country. But these same precepts, when stripped of emotion as well as of ethics, and applied in cold blood to any and all types of "struggle," fall well below the standards of conduct of the hypothetical "man of goodwill." Kotarbiński's own considerable distaste is made clear. The Polish philosopher, himself the author of papers on ethics, has explicitly withheld his own endorsement from the practices he has listed, "since what may be good from the praxeological point of view may be justly condemned on ethical grounds."[16] His chapter on the technique of conflict begins and ends with protestations that what is important is to understand the ruses he describes in order to avoid being surprised and defeated by an unscrupulous opponent.

An element of parodox regarding conflict has attracted the attention of several scholars, among them Kotarbiński, although none, perhaps, has been more strongly attracted than the German sociologist Georg Simmel (1858–1918). The paradoxical statement was a favorite pedagogical device with Simmel, who used it habitually to shake up students' presuppositions and sharpen their critical faculties. In his discussion of conflict, however, Simmel's intention appears less to dazzle his audience than to expound his conviction that human life is inextricably enmeshed in a basic dualism.[17] Thus, without denying the destructive potential of conflict, Simmel calls attention to an essentially integrative function that it performs. In his view life oscillates constantly between such opposing tendencies as love-hate, cooperation-competition, harmony-discord, and the like. If the whole is to have any shape, if it is "to really *be* the whole," Simmel insists, then each element in the contrasting pair must be present to some degree, and therefore each is to be viewed as making a positive contribution toward sustaining group relations, always providing that violence is subjected to at least some restrictions. Otherwise, warns Simmel (citing Kant), open conflict would become a war of extermination. He comments in particular upon the need to refrain "at least from assassination, breach of word, and instigation to treason."[18]

Simmel's equilibrium model is outmoded, and in any event is unlikely to be persuasive to a generation that has been taught that apathy, not hate, is the true opposite of love. It is nevertheless a useful exercise to overturn entrenched notions and recognize that conflict can perform certain integrative functions. For example, a conflict situation can be expected to lead to a study of the adversary, from which might arise eventually an increase in mutual understanding. (The first by-product might equally well be an increase in misunderstanding, depending upon the degree of objectivity animating the study.) Where contact between peoples had previously been slight, it is also conceivable that understanding would in the end be better promoted through open conflict than through "peaceful coexistence," if the latter had been based primarily on ignorance combined with indifference.

But these insights do not of themselves carry us very far. It is unreasonable to expect integration to arise automatically from conflict. Questions concerning the nature of the issue, the intensity and duration of the conflict, and the manner in which conflict is conducted would all need to be taken into consideration.

Kotarbiński's interest in paradox centers upon the paradoxical element inherent in praxeological directives. For example, the element of surprise is a special case of deception. It can take the form of deliberately deviating from what would normally be considered the rational course in order to confound the adversary's plans, which would be based upon the expectation of rational behavior. However, it can also take the form of telling one's true intentions, thereby confusing the adversary who, not knowing what to believe, may either be deceived or be led to adopt a course of action that could more readily be foreseen and hence forestalled.[19]

Similarly, the concept of retreat (which Kotarbiński generalizes as an evasion of struggle in such a way as to change the circumstances in which the opponent finds himself, with the intention of "ensnaring" him), also contains an element of paradox, in that retreat can serve the purpose of attack. A literal example is calculated flight. Metaphorical examples include nonappearance before a given jury, refusal to consent to the date of a trial, and rejection of the nomination of members of a court of arbitration.[20]

Even the most basic praxeological directive—"make the opponent's position as difficult as possible"—contains a paradox. For if the adversary's difficulties are sufficiently increased the result may be that these very pressures will compel the adversary to seek ever more ingenious ways of coping with his problems, to his ultimate advantage.

If we apply praxeological thinking to the conflict between nation states we find that agonology, at least in the hands of the Polish philosopher, becomes in large part a defensive strategy to be employed against an enemy assumed to be, by comparison with one's own side, richer, stronger, and less scrupulous. For praxeological formulations geared to offensive military strategy we turn from the philosopher to the strategist General André Beaufre, who has given special attention to types of strategy and the conditions under which each is appropriate.[23] I have abstracted the following chart from his illuminating discussion. (The strategies listed in this chart are typical rather than exhaustive, and are presented in very broad terms. However, the selection was Beaufre's own and the circumstances governing applicability cover a wide variety of cases. For the subtleties of Beaufre's strategic thinking his treatise should be consulted.)

SELECTED STRATEGIES AND THEIR USES

Typical Patterns of Strategy	Appropriate Circumstances		
	Resources	*Freedom of Action*	*Importance of Issue*
1. Direct threat (deterrent strategy)	Large	Large	Moderate
2. Indirect pressure	Large	Limited by deterrent	Moderate
3. Successive actions combining (1) and (2) with limited application of force	Limited	Restricted	Major, but each episode *appears* to be minor
4. Protracted conflict at low level of intensity	Limited, but *moral* commitment strong	Large	Major, and far greater than for opponent
5. Violent conflict aiming at *rapid* and *complete* military victory	Large	Large	Major, but less than completely vital to opponent

It is of interest to note that two of the five strategies employ credible threats rather than overt violence, two employ violence sparingly, and the fifth, which is characterized by violence, can be assured of success only if victory can be both rapid and complete. The conditions suitable for Maoist strategy—protracted conflict at a low level of intensity—are, it should be added, the same as those appropriate for satyagraha. Granted that these conditions exist and remain stable—the major factor would appear to be the strength of the moral commitment—both types of protracted struggle would appear to have an excellent chance of prevailing eventually, unless defeated in an early stage through an overwhelming use of force. An interesting question arises as to the probable outcome if protracted war of the Maoist variety were to be confronted by satyagraha. The chart suggests that if the issues were equally important to both sides and each had the requisite freedom of action, victory should accrue to the side with the stronger moral commitment. One suspects that much might depend on leadership. The chart, of course, presupposes a praxeological framework throughout, and tacitly assumes leadership of roughly comparable competence.

All struggle, unless it is abruptly terminated, rapidly takes on a "dialectical" quality. In a political or military struggle the "move" may not shift from one side to the other with the set formality of a game or sport, but contingency planning must always take into account the probable range of responses to be expected from the opponent to each move that one makes. The problems of leadership under a "truth" strategy would differ enormously from those facing leadership operating a strategy based upon deceit. Beaufre has graphically portrayed the task of the strategist as he sees it: "the strategist is like a surgeon called upon to operate upon a sick person who is growing continuously and with extreme rapidity and of whose detailed anatomy he is not sure; his operating table is in a state of perpetual motion and he must have ordered the instruments he is to use five years beforehand."[24]

The task for a leader like Gandhi would be incomparably simpler. Since it is an integral part of satyagraha to employ only ethical means and to make all plans public, he would have no problems with security. Neither would he worry overmuch about specific ends, since it is an article of faith that he could be confident of the results provided his means were kept pure. He would escape the problems associated with weaponry but would require a high caliber of human material, with a trained corps of secondary leaders. The satyagraha leader would also be completely free of the predicament lamented by Beaufre: that the praxeological strategist must these days devise a total strategy, but one which is also totally instrumental in the service of policy, which must be left largely to his superiors. Further, to be truly effective policy should be the expression of an underlying philosophy which in Beaufre's experience was all too often lacking. For a leader like Gandhi, strategy in a very real sense *is* philosophy. His attention as commander-in-chief, once the issue was clear, would be focused mainly on two things: making sure that his followers maintained the high standards set for them and bringing his persuasive powers to bear upon the most highly placed of his opponents, preferably through man-to-man contact.

By "a leader like Gandhi" is meant a leader with a firm belief in nonviolence who cherishes such values as truth and honor. Nourishing Gandhi the man in his extraordinary career were dreams he had concerning India, whose "mission," in his belief, was no less than to show mankind how to rid itself of the scourge of war. In his personal life he strove to make himself worthy to lead India in the fulfillment of this high mission.

During the Second World War, as the Japanese forces approached India, Gandhi was able to muster wide support for the demand that the British "quit India" immediately. He stood nearly alone, however, in urging that the country should then rely solely on satyagraha for its defense. He expected that once the British had withdrawn, one of two things would happen. Either the Japanese, seeing that no enemy forces were left there, would leave India alone, or they would attempt to take over India. In the latter, rather more probable case, India would have the opportunity, hopefully under his leadership, of demonstrating the potential which he saw in satyagraha. His plans were predicated upon the avoidance of all violence and rejected any scorched-earth policy.

The course of events was much more commonplace, but Gandhi still retained the hope that India, once freedom was achieved, would base its national defense upon satyagraha. Again he was doomed to disappointment—a disappointment shared by idealists elsewhere. If India, even under the leadership of men Gandhi had himself selected, dared not give his ideals a trial, what were the chances elsewhere for a test of nonviolence as a substitute for war?

The argument for recourse to war when a nation or a civilization is faced with a threat to its values or its very existence is indeed seemingly unanswerable. But neither is there an answer to the argument that as weapons grow increasingly destructive, a resort to warfare poses a serious threat to the civilization it is intended to protect. Can this dilemma be resolved?

A cautiously qualified optimism is currently being expressed in several quarters that the frightfulness of the alternative will yet induce mankind to turn toward nonviolence. The search for "acceptable passage between the horns of our dilemma" led H. J. N. Horsburgh, of the Moral Philosophy Department in the University of Glasgow, to reexamine the claims of Gandhian satyagraha as a moral equivalent of war.[25] Few would disagree with his conclusion that nonviolence is much superior to violence in its effect upon the way of life to be defended. He is also able to make a persuasive case for considering nonviolence as at least not inferior to violence in effectiveness as measured by several important criteria, including the one upon which mankind is now so heavily staking its future—the ability to deter aggression. He sees no prospect that Gandhian satyagraha can hope to play an important role in determining the relations between nation states, but sees reason to expect that nations will turn toward a non-Gandhian type of nonviolence, that is, one based upon expedience. (This interesting and important study has much more to offer than can be indicated here. It deserves the careful attention of anyone interested in exploring the relative claims to effectiveness of violence and nonviolence.)

War does indeed seem now to be widely regarded with loathing. Conflict, however, is quite another matter and can most certainly not be eliminated. Is Kotarbiński not correct in holding that "struggle" (as opposed to warfare) should not be renounced because mankind needs the spur of the compulsory situation, indeed "needs threats to life and to those values without which life is not worth living?" His reading of history has convinced him that whenever such threats have ceased, stagnation sets in; people become "mere consumers," and their vigor atrophies. Men, in his striking phrase, are "like deep-water fish—accustomed to strong external pressure, so when they reach shallow water they perish, burst by internal forces."[26]

Warfare does provide such pressure. Is there a source, apart from war, which might provide it? Certainly Kotarbiński's own recommendation for "taming" struggle by channeling it into competition in sports, the arts, and industrial production does not meet his own requirements with respect to the need for threats against life and cherished values. It was once suggested that only an invasion from another planet could turn earth's population away from internecine strife. That hope—if hope it was —has proved illusory.

As the destructive potential not merely of warfare but also of the very technology on which we have long prided ourselves becomes ever clearer, mankind's dilemma grows sharper and the intractable questions require rephrasing. The question no longer is: can mankind abolish war? It goes even beyond: can warfare indeed abolish man? For some it becomes: does man's technology indeed pose a threat to the continued existence of human life on this planet? To many the answer to that question seems self-evident and they ask most urgently: can man be brought to realize the full extent of his predicament and take remedial action before the process of environmental deterioration becomes irreversible? These overriding, global questions bring us back to time-worn problems of intergroup conflict, but with a keener snese of urgency. The "compulsory situation" that Kotarbiński posits as essential to progress is now upon us, for we are confronted with a possibly fatal environmental crisis. Questions about the potential of weapons technology to destroy human life on the planet become intertwined with the even greater considerations of technological man's capacity to destroy his life-sustaining environment.

Faced with so dire a predicament the relative merits of competing modes for conducting conflict require profound reconsideration. At one extreme is the praxeological nightmare so graphically set forth by General Beaufre (p. 195). Here the *potential* for violence is staggering, despite the explicit desire that it need never be employed. At the other extreme is the Gandhian solution, the product of a social philosophy as profoundly ethical as his novel technique for conducting overt conflict, a solution that looked to the eventual abolition of all "machinery." (This was of course an utterly unattainable goal, presenting Gandhi with many problems. He did not classify such devices as handlooms as machinery, and even urged the development of improved looms. He also jocularly granted temporary exemption to the printing press used in the publication of his attack upon other machinery!)

Where both these extremes are at fault, it would appear, is in failing to make appropriate utilization of science and technology. The Gandhian approach all but ignores science; the praxeological approach misuses it in continuing to devote excessive time, treasure, and human ingenuity to the development of weapons systems and industrial products that compound the magnitude of the environmental threat to human existence. It will not do to either ignore or misuse science. For science *is* "intrinsically more revolutionary than any ideology or political or social movement," as Roy Finch points out [p. 35].

How then should we use science in these troubled times, when dissatisfaction abounds and the rumbles of a revolutionary groundswell portend imminent change? Today a rather hybrid form of praxeological thinking dominates approaches to conflict and to technologically generated environmental problems. Are we to move toward a more rigorous—and dehumanized—praxeology, or can we, through the mediation of science, develop a humanistic praxeology which can accommodate certain insights developed through the Gandhian approach? A step in this direction could be taken by redefining the central praxeological concept of "efficiency."

It is significant that the praxeological approach as developed by Kotarbinski with a *nonaffluent* society in mind displays a tendency to favor nonviolent means as more "efficient" (cheaper). Under conditions of relative affluence, however, efficiency is more likely to be equated with time-saving, thus easily diminishing, if not negating, the moderating effect of cost considerations on the escalation of violence. Once escalation has taken place, however, a serious impediment to its reversal arises from the reliance of the praxeological strategist on deceit. The sharpest point of contrast between satyagraha and agonology is not with respect to violence but with respect to "truth."

A philosophy of conflict adequate to our times could well center upon the basic kind of ethical consideration that, in holding that power lay in pursuing and asserting truth, led to the development of satyagraha. In calling for an effort to "understand the *objective* nature of morality," Roy Finch expresses the belief that to do so will require a "vast upheaval of thought, which has scarcely begun" [p. 33]. Such a beginning, I would contend, was made by Gandhi, who also extended it further to an understanding (and application) of the *uses* of morality in situations of conflict.

In the "recycling" of ideas that bear upon the moral facets of our predicament, we would do well to discard outworn political doctrines. Seductive promises of inevitably assured ends seem currently to be effecting the rehabilitation of theories of conflict built into deterministic political philosophies and social ideologies —and this despite a long record of betrayal of humanistic impulses. Slogans such as "power to the people," as past experience indicates, can all too readily lead to the exploitation of the aggrieved by an abrasive handful who give primacy to politics and ideology over human values. Is not the true "power of the people" to be defined in terms of the building up of moral courage to the point where the majority of the people become immune both to threats of violence and to the temptation to indulge in violent acts?

To suggest that we begin with Gandhian nonviolence and satyagraha, that we supplement it with a redefinition of "efficiency," and that we make science serve a constructively creative purpose is to present a new set of intellectual and practical problems. But today's generation cannot lightly dismiss the possibility, whatever the odds, that in their lifetime our planet may become incapable of further supporting human life. A way must be found to direct the revolutionary potential of our science into ecology-oriented systems in which conflict theory takes its own innovative place. The essentially human process involved in that effort could not only avert catastrophe but also usher in a new renaissance.

NOTES

1. For Gandhi's autobiographical writings see his *Satyagraha in South Africa,* available in several editions of which the most useful is in *The Collected Works of Mahatma Gandhi* (New Delhi: Government of India, Publications Division, 1968) vol. 29, pp. xviii–269; and *The Story of My Experiments with Truth* (Washington, D.C.: Public Affairs Press, 1948).
2. See Tadeusz Kotarbiński, *Gnosiology: The Scientific Approach to Knowledge* (New York: Pergamon Press, 1966), translated from the revised Polish edition (Warsaw, 1961) of a work first published in 1929.
3. See particularly Joan V. Bondurant, *Conquest of Violence: The Gandhian Philosophy of Conflict,* rev. ed. (Berkeley: University of California Press, 1965), (1st ed. Princeton University Press, 1958); and her article "Satyagraha versus Duragraha: The Limits of Symbolic Violence," in *Gandhi: His Relevance for Our Times,* ed. G. Ramachandran and T. K. Mahadevan, 2d ed. (New Delhi: Gandhi Peace Foundation, 1967), pp. 99–112.
4. Tadeusz Kotarbiński, *Praxiology: An Introduction to the Sciences of Efficient Action* (New York: Pergamon Press, 1965), (first Polish edition 1955). English and American spelling fluctuates between praxiology and praxeology. I have adopted Norman Bailey's suggestion and have used praxeology except in citing the title of the English translation of this book.
5. Norman A. Bailey, "Toward a Praxeological Theory of Conflict," *Orbis,* XI, no. 4 (Winter 1968), 1081–1112.
6. Kotarbiński cites an edition in German, *Kampf* (New York, 1907). Lasker's remarkable success is generally attributed to his ability to discover and exploit the temperamental weaknesses of his opponents through close study of their games.
7. Kotarbiński, *Praxiology,* p. 7.
8. *Ibid.,* p. 12.
9. *Ibid.,* p. 13.
10. From Gandhi's speech on the Noncooperation Resolution, at the Calcutta Congress, September 8, 1920 (*Collected Works,* vol. 28, p. 246).
11. *Satyagraha in South Africa,* p. xiv.
12. See his speech of 13 August 1924 in his *Collected Works,* vol. 25, pp. 56–63.

13. Written to a friend in February 1946. D. G. Tendulkar, *Mahatma: Life of Mohandas Karamchand Gandhi* (Bombay: Vithalbhai K. Jhaveri and D. G. Tendulkar, 1953), vol. 7, pp. 84–85.
14. Bondurant, *Conquest of Violence*, chap. 2.
15. Kotarbiński, *Praxiology*, chap. 13.
16. *Ibid.*, p. 159.
17. Georg Simmel, *Conflict*, trans. Kurt H. Wolff, and *The Web of Group-Affiliations*, trans. Reinhard Bendix (Glencoe, Ill.: Free Press, 1955), pp. 13 ff.
18. *Ibid.*, p. 26.
19. Kotarbiński, *Praxiology*, pp. 170–171.
20. *Ibid.*, pp. 171–172.
21. *Ibid.*, p. 174.
22. *Ibid.*, p. 206.
23. André Beaufre, *An Introduction to Strategy* (London: Faber and Faber, 1965), pp. 26–30. (First published in France by Armand Colin under the auspices of the Centre d'Etudes de Politique Etrangere, in 1963.) General Beaufre's long and varied experience includes serving as French representative on the NATO Standing Group in Washington.
24. *Ibid.*, p. 46.
25. H. J. N. Horsburgh, *Nonviolence and Aggression: A Study of Gandhi's Moral Equivalent of War* (London, New York, Toronto, Bombay: Oxford University Press, 1968).
26. Kotarbiński, *Praxiology*, p. 193.
27. Gandhi, "Hind Swaraj" or "Indian Home Rule," *Collected Works*, vol. 10, pp. 6–68.

Index

Abbott, T. K., 61
Accommodation, as mechanism of
    nonviolent action, 156
Action, nonviolent
    cases of, 163–169
    methods of, 154–155
    technique of, 151–171
    violence versus, 156–158
Acton, Lord, 24
African resistance movements, 100–
    101
Agonology, 184, 185, 189, 191, 200
    directives, 190
    objective of, 190
Anarchism, 55, 65
Apology (Plato), 50, 61, 62, 69
Arendt, Hannah, 3, 4, 23, 99, 108
Aristotle, 185
Arthashastra, 184
Aufricht, Hans, 107

Bahehot, Walter, 3
Bailey, Norman, 184, 201
Baker, Russell, 174
Ballots, 81
Beaufre, André, 194, 195, 196, 199,
    202
Bendix, Reinhard, 202

Benz, Carl, 112
Berkman, Alexander, 31–32, 44
Bloch, Marc, 93, 107
Bondurant, Joan V., 108, 184, 189,
    201, 202
    Creative Conflict and the Limits
        of Symbolic Violence, 120–
        132
    Search for a Theory of Conflict,
        The, 1–25

Carter, April, 171
Case, Clarence Marsh, 100, 108,
    171
Castro, Fidel, 41–42
Change
    mechanisms of, 155–156
    social, 46
        threat of violence and, 73–87
Chapman, John W., 24
Chappell, V. C., 61
Christ, Jesus, 54, 186
Civil disobedience, 6–7
    moral claim in, limits to the,
        50–61
    moral ground of, 62–69
    nonviolent, 50–61
Civilian defense, 172–179
Clausewitz, Karl von, 3, 101, 108

203

Coercion, nonviolent, 156
Cold War, 37, 38, 41, 42, 43, 77
Committee for Non-Violent Action, 37
Communism, 42
Conflict
    creative, 122–126
        dynamics of, 123–126
    fractionating, 135–150
        comments on, 146–150
    theory of, search for a, 1–22
Confrontation, 97, 101
Constitutionalism, 86
Conversion, as mechanism of nonviolent action, 155–156
Conway, Frank MacIvor, 23, 26
Creative conflict, 122–126
    dynamics of, 123–126
Crito (Plato), 50, 63, 69
Crozier, Brian, 107

Daniels, Dan, 171
Defense, civilian, 172–179
Defoe, Daniel, 185
Demonstrations, peaceable, 86
Despotism, 55
Dewey, John, 124
Dickson, W. P., 108
Dictatorships, 85
Diwakar, Ranganath R., 171
Domestic process, and threat of violence, 84–87

Eichmann, Adolf, 32
Elkins, Stanley, 98, 108
Ellington, James, 61
Emerson, Ralph Waldo, 189
Erikson, Erik, 122, 132
Evolution, 111–119
    social, 115–116

Fellowship of Reconciliation, 37
Finch, Roy, 4, 5, 199, 200
    New Peace Movement, The, 29–43
Finkelstein, Lawrence, 10
    Comments on "Fractionating Conflict," 146–150
Fisher, Margaret, 12, 24
    Contrasting Approaches to Conflict, 183–201
Fisher, Roger, 10
    Fractionating Conflict, 135–145
        comments on, 146–150

Fractionating conflict, 135–150
French Revolution, 112–113
Freud, Sigmund, 14
Frick, Henry, 31–32
Friedrich, C. J., 108, 132

Gandhi, Mohandus, 9, 22, 29–30, 50, 123, 128, 131, 161–162, 164, 165, 184–191, 195–197, 199, 200, 201, 202

Hardman, J. B. S., 108
Hartmann, Heinz, 24–25
Hiller, E. T., 171
Hitler, Adolf, 32, 141, 176
Hobbes, Thomas, 3, 65, 103, 108
Hoffman, Stanley, 23
Hoggett, David, 171
Horsburgh, H. J. N., 197, 202
Huizinga, Jan, 93, 107
Hume, David, 46
Hume, Portia Bell, 24, 132

Industrial Revolution, 112
International Court of Justice, 145
International relations, 82–84
    fractionating conflict and, 135–150
Intervention, nonviolent, 154–155
Intimidation, 98
Isolationism, 48

Jones, Ernest, 5, 9–10, 13
    Evolution and Revolution, 111–119
Jones, Mervyn, 113

Kant, Immanuel, 3, 59, 61, 192
Khrushchev, Nikita, 33
King, Martin Luther, Jr., 3
Kotarbiński, Tadeusz, 184–186, 189, 191, 192–193, 197–199, 201, 202
Kuper, Leo, 100, 108

La Fontaine, Jean de, 185
Lapp, Ralph E., 44
Lasker, Emanuel, 185, 201
Lasswell, Harold, 18–19, 24
Laws, 79–82
Lawson, James, 47
Leviathan (Hobbes), 103, 108
Liddell Hart, B. H., 158, 171
Ligt, Barthelemy de, 171

MacArthur, Douglas, 44
Machiavelli, 3
Mahadevan, T. K., 171, 201
Malcolm, Norman, 61
Mannheim, Karl, 87
Manyon, L. A., 107
Marx, Karl, 185
Mau Mau, 100
McNeil, William H., 24
Mommsen, Theodor, 98, 108
Munich, lessons learned from, 141
Muste, A. J., 47
Mysticism, 15

Naess, Arne, 122
Nations, 79
Negro student movement, 47
Negroes, 47
Niebuhr, Reinhold, 47
Nieburg, H. L., 8
    Threat of Violence and Social
        Change, The, 73–87
Nietzsche, Friedrich, 117
Noncooperation, nonviolent, 154
Nonviolence
    action and, 151–171
    civil disobedience, 50–69
    modes of, 27–69
    pacifism, new, 45–49
    peace movement and, 29–43
Nonviolent action
    cases of, 163–169
    methods of, 154–155
    technique of, 151–171
    violence versus, 156–158
Nuclear weapons, development of,
        peace movement and, 36–37

Oliver, Edmund H., 108
O'Neill, Eugene, 77
Oppenheimer, Heinrich, 108
Overkill, 35

Pacifism, 4–6
    new, 45–49
Park, Richard L., 132
Parsons, Talcott, 18, 24, 25, 185
Pattison, M., 24
Peace movement, new, 29–43
Peace societies, history of, 29–43
Peacemakers, 37
Pennock, J. Roland, 24
Pickus, Robert, 23

Plato, 50, 61, 62, 69
Politics, 79
    international, 82–84
Poujade, M., 178
Power
    opponent's, indirect approach to,
        158–160
    social, 46, 47
Praxeology, 184–185, 193, 199
Prison Memoirs of an Anarchist
        (Berkman), 31, 44
Prosch, Harry, 6, 62
    Limits to the Moral Claim in
        Civil Disobedience, 50–61
Protest, nonviolent, 154
Psychopathology and Politics (Lass-
        well), 19
Punishment, violence and, 98, 101–
        105

Quakers, 161, 166

Radicalism, 31
Radin, Paul, 107
Ramachandran, G., 171, 201
Repression, 14
Resistance, violence and, 96–100
Revolution, 111–119
    material, 111, 112
    political, 111
    social, 111, 112–113
Roberts, Adam, 151, 171, 172
Robinson Crusoe (Defoe), 185
Roe, Ann, 15, 24
Roheim, Geza, 25
Rousseau, Jean Jacques, 3
Rucker, Darnell, 6–7
    Moral Ground of Civil Disobe-
        dience, The, 62–69
Russian Revolution, (1917), 112–
        113

Santayana, George, 16
Satyagraha, 9, 10, 12, 15, 16, 20,
        100, 122–123, 130, 131,
        161, 183–191, 196–197, 200
    directives, 190
    dynamics involved in, 123–126
    objective of, 123, 190
Schelling, Thomas, 11
    Some Questions on Civilian De-
        fense, 172–179
Self-awareness, 15

Shaka, 94
Sharp, Gene, 11
   Technique of Nonviolent Action,
      The, 151–171
Shaw, Bernard, 113
Shils, Edward A., 24, 25
Sibley, Mulford Q., 172, 179
Simmel, Georg, 24, 97, 107, 192
Singer, J. David, 132
Singer, Kurt, 24
Slavery, 98–99
Social change, 46
   threat of violence and, 73–87
Social power, 46, 47
Socrates, 50, 62–63, 67, 186
Sorel, Georges, 3
Spitz, David, 23
Stalin, Joseph, 32, 33
Stampp, Kenneth, 98, 108
Stevenson, Charles, 58, 61
Strikes, 124
Symbolic violence, 7–11, 109–132
   limits of, 120–132
   nature of, 126–128

Tendulkar, D. G., 202
Terror, concept of, 90–93
Terrorism, 31, 89–107
Terrorism and Communism (Trot-
      sky), 31, 44
Thernstrom, Stephan, 5
   New Pacifism, The, 45–49
Tillich, Paul, 94, 107
Tinker, Irene, 132
Tolman, Edward C., 25
Totalitarianism, 84–85
Tradition, continuity of, 119
Trotsky, Leon, 31, 32, 44
Tsarism, 31

United Nations, 145

Varro, Marcus Terentius, 99, 108
Versailles Treaty, 149
Vigilantism, 80
Violence, 7–11
   alternatives to, 10–11, 133–179
   definition of, 87
   forms of, 71–107
   international, threat of, 83
   nonviolent action versus, 156–158
   process of terror and, 89–107
   punishment and, 98, 101–105
   resistance and, 95–100
   symbolic, 7–11, 109–132
      limits of, 120–132
      nature of, 126–128
   threat of, social change and, 73–
      87
   uses of, 71–107
   war and, 100–101
Voting, 82

Walter, Eugene V., 8, 9, 23, 24
   Violence and the Process of Ter-
      ror, 89–107
Waltz, Kenneth, 23
Walzer, Michael, 47
War, 35–38
   violence and, 100–101
War Resisters League, 37
Watkins, Frederick, 17–18, 24
Wittgenstein, Ludwig, 61
Wolfers, Arnold, 23
Wolff, Kurt H., 107, 202
Wright, Quincy, 3

Yalem, Roland J., 23
Young, Roland, 24